"This latest of Richard Wood's books on narcissism promises to be his masterpiece. For a small book, it is one of the most comprehensive and engaging reviews of narcissism that I have read. Wood has covered most of the authoritative contributors to the study of narcissism, and I would think that this book would be the go-to book for psychiatric residents, psychoanalytic candidates, and even the journalistic world. Congratulations on a fine piece of work."

David Ray Freebury, MB Ch FICPC DLFAPA,
training and supervising analyst, Canadian
and Toronto psychoanalytic societies

"Richard Wood leads us into the complex, sometimes confusing, world of narcissism. Summarizing seminal contributions, he weighs in on seemingly contradictory elements, providing useful reflections. He relates these matters to his experience with narcissistic patients and parents, with thought-provoking things to say about the relationships that narcissists and those who suffered narcissistic parenting attempt to establish. These ideas will stimulate readers not only with respect to patients but also regarding clinical theory and the wider sociopolitical world (e.g., relationships between grandiose narcissistic leaders and their supporters)."

Brent Willock, author,
Comparative-Integrative Psychoanalysis

"Dr. Wood's latest book is an exceptional integration of clinical research, theory and practice on the subject and treatment of narcissism in its various forms. What emerges is a ground-breaking model through which this condition can best be understood and more completely recognized.

Dr. Wood acknowledges the work of his co-navigators and renders a great service by articulating their insights ... untangling the cross-threads of past and present clinical experience. The dynamics of narcissism have never been so compellingly described."

Tim Gilmor, Ph.D., specializing in
personality/clinical psychology

"Dr. Richard Wood provides us with another well-written and engaging book exploring narcissism. Wood first offers an impressive and well-digested literature review of contemporary perspectives of thin-skinned, or vulnerable narcissism, and thick-skinned, or grandiose narcissism. After providing a number of useful clinical examples he expounds his own perspective. Wood understands narcissism as a defense meant to protect the psyche from unbearable and catastrophic outcomes. Wood does not see thin-skinned narcissism as falling within the spectrum of narcissistic disorders. He views thin-skinned narcissistic patients as suffering from cumulative developmental post-traumatic stress. These vulnerable people were invaded and tormented by malignant narcissistic early relational experiences with vampire-like narcissistic parents who have damaged their souls. Wood views these traumatized patients as quite amenable to psychodynamic treatment. The book will therefore support psychotherapists and psychoanalysts who are willing to discover the deeply traumatized person underneath the label of 'narcissist.' Dr. Wood also throws light on the pathological relationship between malignant narcissistic leaders and their exploited followers. The book is a significant contribution to our field and a gift to all of us."

Era A. Loewenstein, Ph.D., training and supervising analyst, San Francisco Center for Psychoanalysis, editor of the *Psychoanalytic Inquiry* Issue: *Perspectives on Populist and Fascistic States of Mind* (Taylor and Francis, 2023)

Narcissism

Narcissism: A Contemporary Introduction provides a historical overview of this key foundational concept within psychoanalytic thought.

Richard Wood offers a critical overview of the theoretical landscape that characterizes the understanding of narcissism, referring to the work of Fromm, Rosenfeld, Kernberg, and Kohut, among others. He delineates and investigates three key forms of narcissism: severe, pathological narcissism that can result in extreme human suffering; narcissism that falls within the spectrum of Narcissistic Personality Disorder; and healthy forms of narcissism that are essential to successful personal, cultural, and creative development.

Using clinical examples throughout, Wood aids psychoanalysts and psychologists in training and practice in recognizing, evaluating, and treating patients with narcissistic personality traits. His thorough and jargon-free approach will also support students looking for a comprehensive overview of narcissism.

Richard Wood is a registered psychologist in the province of Ontario, Canada. He is a founding member of the Canadian Association of Psychologists in Disability Assessment (CAPDA) and is the author of *A Study of Malignant Narcissism: Personal and Professional Insights* (2022).

Routledge Introductions to Contemporary Psychoanalysis

Aner Govrin, Ph.D.
Series Editor

Yael Peri Herzovich, Ph.D.
Executive Editor

Itamar Ezer
Assistant Editor

"Routledge Introductions to Contemporary Psychoanalysis" is one of the prominent psychoanalytic publishing ventures of our day. It will comprise dozens of books that will serve as concise introductions dedicated to influential concepts, theories, leading figures, and techniques in psychoanalysis covering every important aspect of psychoanalysis.

The length of each book is fixed at 40,000 words.

The series' books are designed to be easily accessible to provide informative answers in various areas of psychoanalytic thought. Each book will provide updated ideas on topics relevant to contemporary psychoanalysis – from the unconscious and dreams, projective identification and eating disorders, through neuropsychoanalysis, colonialism, and spiritual-sensitive psychoanalysis. Books will also be dedicated to prominent figures in the field, such as Melanie Klein, Jaque Lacan, Sandor Ferenczi, Otto Kernberg, and Michael Eigen.

Not serving solely as an introduction for beginners, the purpose of the series is to offer compendiums of information on particular topics within different psychoanalytic schools. We ask authors to review a topic but also address the readers with their own personal views and contributions to the specific chosen field. Books will make intricate ideas comprehensible without compromising their complexity.

We aim to make contemporary psychoanalysis more accessible to both clinicians and the general educated public.

Aner Govrin – Editor

The Death Drive: A Contemporary Introduction
Rossella Valdrè

Narcissism: A Contemporary Introduction
Richard Wood

Narcissism

A Contemporary Introduction

Richard Wood

Routledge
Taylor & Francis Group

LONDON AND NEW YORK

Designed cover image: Michal Heiman, Asylum 1855–2020, *The Sleeper* (video, psychoanalytic sofa and Plate 34), exhibition view, Herzliya Museum of Contemporary Art, 2017

First published 2025
by Routledge
4 Park Square, Milton Park, Abingdon, Oxon OX14 4RN

and by Routledge
605 Third Avenue, New York, NY 10158

Routledge is an imprint of the Taylor & Francis Group, an informa business

British Library Cataloguing-in-Publication Data
A catalogue record for this book is available from the British Library

ISBN: 978-1-032-64952-8 (hbk)
ISBN: 978-1-032-64951-1 (pbk)
ISBN: 978-1-032-64953-5 (ebk)

DOI: 10.4324/9781032649535

Typeset in Times New Roman
by KnowledgeWorks Global Ltd.

To my magical wife, Mary, and an inspiring
little presence called Arabella

Contents

Acknowledgments

My first acknowledgment must be to my wife. She gave up our time together, offered endless encouragement to persevere in the face of a challenging project, endured my varied frustrations, and, finally, proofread my work and tested it for readability. Patience, thy name is Mary. I also offer thanks to my editor, Aner Govrin, of Routledge's Introduction to Contemporary Psychoanalysis series. Your patience and support, too, were immensely appreciated. You managed to get through your work in a very timely fashion in the midst of the maelstrom that, tragically, is now Israel and the Middle East. I also have my three stalwart colleagues to thank who act as editors of my work upon whom I can always depend for honest, thoroughgoing appraisals of my work – Drs Tim Gilmor, D. Ray Freebury, and Brent Willock. And finally, I am deeply indebted to the many pioneering clinicians who preceded me who built the foundations upon which this book rests.

Chapter 1

A Confusing and Elusive Concept

When I faced the task of capturing essential psychoanalytic conceptions of narcissism, I admit that I felt intimidated, particularly because I would be trying to do so within a 40,000 word limit – a constraint that I knew would be daunting to work within the face of so many rich and variegated ideas. Rendering this challenge even more imposing was the enduring confusion within the psychoanalytic world about what we mean by the term narcissism. Consider, for example, Freud's retrospective appraisal of his early construction of narcissism:

> "The narcissism" had a difficult labour and bears all the marks of a corresponding deformation. (Freud's appreciation of his initial attempts to define narcissism – see)

Over half a century later Judith Teicholz provided a similar assessment:

> Freud's ideas on narcissism contain contradictions, inconsistencies, and gaps, which are still being struggled with in the current decade.
> (Teicholz, 1978, p. 833 citing Pulver, 1970; Stolorow, 1975)

Did greater clarity emerge with the passage of years as other theorists contributed their ideas or expanded upon some of Freud's and each other's musings about narcissism?

> ...by all accounts narcissism is a pivotal psychoanalytic concept and yet it is by no means clear how the concept can be

DOI: 10.4324/9781032649535-1

unproblematically integrated with other significant branches of psychoanalytic metatheory.... The place of narcissism has become even more unsettled in the wake of theoretical and technical innovations since Freud's death while its importance has, paradoxically, grown... The theory of narcissism is a vast and convoluted topic.

(Smith, 1988, pp. 302–303)

Of the many concepts that Freud bequeathed us, few have proved as elusive as narcissism.

(Auerbach, 1990, p. 545)

By becoming such an overinclusive concept, narcissism is in danger of losing its theoretical and clinical specificity.

(Taylor, 1992, cited in Lester, 2000, p. 87)

(The concept of narcissism) has been used clinically to denote sexual perversion and genetically to denote a stage of development with particular characteristics. In reference to relationships it is also been used to denote a type of object choice and a mode of relating to the environment. Finally it has been used to denote various aspects of clinical states of self-esteem.

(Meissner 2008, referencing the work of Pulver (1970) and Moore (1975))

Meisner pointed out that Pulver went on to identify several subtypes of narcissism, including a developmental stage, a form of object choice, a mode of relating, a self-referential attitude, a posture reflecting opposition to object love, and one that both reinforced and supported object love (Meissner, 2008, p. 464). Meisner further noted that Moore "argued for the retention of the global term in spite of the confusion that attended the concept of narcissism – an organizing matrix for theoretical construction covering the wide variety of forms" (Meissner, 2008, p. 464).

"Narcissism remains difficult to theorize. Multiple psychoanalytic perspectives have brought richness and depth to the concept, but have produced a somewhat confusing and muddled literature" (Kealy & Ogrudniczuk, 2014, p. 102 citing the work of Britton (2004)). Later in the same paper, they note: "Despite widespread colloquial use of the

term, narcissism remains a notoriously simple slippery construct..."
(p. 103)

Hinze reflected that "(we use the words narcissism and narcissistic)
to describe normal or deviant psychological phenomena... They are so
widespread and often so loosely used that they seem to have lost their
descriptive and discriminatory power" (Hinze, 2017, pp. 20–21).

Why, indeed, have we found it so difficult to settle upon a consensus
about narcissism?

I would argue that narcissism has felt so insurmountable because
psychoanalytic science is still relatively nascent in spite of the extraordinary efforts practitioners have made to understand the human
condition. Perhaps more so than other branches of science, the job of
understanding ourselves and other people requires us to immerse ourselves in all of the messiness, all of the contradictions, and all of the
dark corners of our souls – aspects of ourselves that we can experience
as terribly disconcerting and even terrifying to explore. We often find
ourselves unintentionally limited by both conscious and unconscious
fears of what we might discover. As we are learning about ourselves, if
we can bear to make this journey, there are wonders to be encountered
and to be celebrated, to be sure, but our determination can be all too
easily derailed by our defenses.

Rendering this work even more difficult is a growing realization
that each of us is defined by our own unique subjectivities and their
own unique sets of dynamics – each person representing complicated,
intricate realities or separate, individual worlds, if one likes – that we
are asking ourselves to try to define and appreciate that interweave
with culture, genetics, brain function, and biochemistry. Endless
worlds colliding and interacting with one another, each of which is
defined by its own specificities but is subject to the impact of its neigh-
bors. It sounds impossible to imagine that we can undertake such work
successfully. As we make our efforts, I would say it is inevitable that
we produce multiplicities of conceptualization – models of human
functioning – that approximate some aspects of the human experience
better than others. That has to be especially true of conceptions like
narcissism that appear to play a foundational role in our grasp of who
we are, as this book will argue. Foundational or keystone concepts
must inevitably intersect with many of the other clinical and theoretical constructions we are in the process of either building or modifying.
As conceptualizations shift and change, so, too, does appreciation of

our seminal ideas – a never-ending dance that renders new landscapes for us to consider.

We're left grappling with many emergent, differing models of "narcissism," then, to choose from, a seeming cacophony of ideas and abstractions that we have to apply as best we can in dealing with the clinical realities we have to contend with in our day-by-day practices. As I did with my first book, I find myself returning to Daniel Shaw's (2013) conception of science as being like a group of blind men and women attempting to divine that part of the elephant that they think they know. As I hope the reader will see, many of our conceptions or models are now supported by rigorous scientific investigation, but no one of them – at least in so far as I can see – allows us to integrate what we know into a single, compelling perspective. Moreover, as you will see as we move through this material, it's not even clear that practitioners who are attempting to understand narcissism are referring to a homogenous group of patients as they describe their discoveries – what one group of clinicians would think of as being narcissistic, in other words, another would not.

Perhaps an example would be helpful.

Otto Kernberg and Heinz Kohut have each made major contributions to the evolution of psychoanalytic thinking about narcissism. While there are some similarities in their formulations (agreement that a defective self is at the core of narcissistic disorders and that archaic or early grandiose self-images and archaic idealized parental images make a significant contribution to adult narcissistic pathology – see Teicholz, 1978), their theoretical positions are largely defined by striking differences in the way that they think about narcissism. Hinze believed that "many analysts would share the idea that at the core of a narcissistic personality, there is an integrated, although highly pathological, grandiose self which Kernberg characterizes in his 1975 work…" (Hinze, 2017, p. 27). The grandiose self provides the narcissistic personality with cohesion and protects it against dependence, neediness, and vulnerability, which it finds unbearable as a result of insults, disappointments, and severe frustrations such a personality has had to endure in the first few years of life (the so-called late oral phase). The cost of investing in the protection that the grandiose self offers is tragic – denial of the best parts of ourselves that might otherwise allow us to build sustaining and life-giving intimacies with others.

The implication of Kernberg's formulation is that people presenting narcissistic personality disorder (NPD) isolate themselves from connection to others, locked up in their own house, as it were, unable to get out and unwilling to let anybody move inside in a meaningful way for very long. Their existence is defined by intractable mistrustfulness. Because such personalities are incapable of tolerating either their own defectiveness or the needs of others, they must, of necessity, devote much of their energy toward endlessly re-confirming their own grandiosity. Denying their imperfections and their need for interdependence places them in the position of muting their humanity and negating their capacity for empathy and compassion. Perceived self-interest predominates. Other people are treated as things that can be used and then discarded. Rapacity and self-aggrandizement, however, are rarely satisfied; they leave the enactor hungry and envious. The grandiose self-structure is fragile and rigid; if grandiosity is pierced or compromised, identity is forfeit and crisis ensues. Central to Kernberg's formulation is the notion that the grandiose self supports itself and consolidates its entitlements through a markedly aggressive interpersonal posture. The inner world of an individual struggling with NPD, particularly in its more extreme forms (malignant narcissism), was thought to be infiltrated and largely defined by idealized representations of the self, "shadows" of the people the narcissist has exploited whose only value lay in their ability to feed him, and dreaded enemies. In a particularly poignant passage in an early paper, Kernberg noted that at the center of the pathological narcissist's being was "the image of a hungry, enraged, empty self, full of impotent anger at being frustrated, and fearful of the world which seems as hateful and revengeful as the patient himself... a worthless, poverty-stricken, empty person who always feels left outside, devoured by envy of those who have food, happiness, and fame" (Kernberg, 1970, p. 57).

The degree to which this wretched state obtains depends upon the levels of hostility that characterize the pathological grandiose self. It also depends upon whether a given narcissistic personality is organized along the lines of what Kernberg and his associates call a higher level, a borderline level, or a level of malignant narcissism, the least favorable disposition for pathological narcissism (Diamond et al., 2022). "Higher" levels of organization imply some capacity for good reality testing, interrelatedness, and stability in the self, while a borderline level of organization is associated with identity diffusion, ego weakness, limited ability to reflect, impaired empathy, and obvious difficulties with love and work. Malignant narcissism, in turn, is described as a state in which paranoid features, vengeful destructiveness, anti-social features, and identification of the self with powerful punitive others become prominent. Please keep in mind as we use the term malignant narcissism throughout this book that it represents a propositional diagnosis, albeit one that has been part of the common currency of clinical language since Fromm coined this term in 1964.

In considering the broad stroke factors, in addition to the formation of a grandiose self, that might contribute to instigation of NPD, the Kernberg group at Cornell identified a number of potential contributors, including temperamental givens, adverse childhood experiences, socio-cultural influences, attachment style, and deficits in emotional as opposed to cognitive empathy (Diamond et al., 2022). As an aside, emotional empathy refers to the capacity to feel another's experience, while cognitive empathy refers to the ability to discern, on an intellectual level, what someone else is feeling without necessarily feeling it oneself. Diamond et al.'s (2022) book provides a very extensive exploration of propositional etiologies that may set the stage for the formation of NPD and a grandiose self.

Shane reflected that the Kernbergian model emphasizes rigid, unyielding systems of defense and withdrawal that need to be actively attacked in treatment (Shane, 2014). In effect, the therapist is charged with prying the patient away from his/her solipsistic existence, his/her hostility, and his/her investment in grandiosity in the face of the patient's envy and his attempts to defeat the therapist. From this perspective, Kernbergian therapy represents a kind of combat in which assertive interpretation of transference hopefully helps the patient free himself from the impoverishment and the solitude that his narcissism creates for him/her. Parenthetically, transference refers to the patient's compulsion to act out destructive relationship patterns with the therapist that have characterized his/her other relationships. Countertransference manifestations (referring to the therapist's own emotional responses to work with the patient) could be expected to be marked by intensity and, oftentimes, by significant discomfort.

Kernberg derived much of his formulation from an object relations perspective; as he underscored in his most recent work (Diamond et al., 2022), central to his appreciation of narcissistic personality were the internal representations of the important dyadic interactions that had defined a given patient's life (again, particularly very early on in life) and that, in turn, gave shape and structure to the patient's inner world. As noted, such dyadic representations could be expected to express themselves in transference interactions just as they did in the pathological narcissist's interactions with other people – interactions that could be seen to be infiltrated with marked hostility and intractable mistrust and cynicism as narcissism became more pronounced.

Kealy and Ogrudniczuk (2014) point out that within a Kernbergian framework, the inability to tolerate interdependence and vulnerability meant that the capacity to genuinely love others was compromised. They also underscored that

> pathological narcissism is not an overinvestment in the self, but a distorted version of the self; it is not a real self that is invested in. How can one love oneself when one's shortcomings, failures, and transgressions cannot be tolerated?...
>
> (Kealy and Ogrodniczuk, 2014, p. 107, referencing Kernberg's (1984) book *Severe Personality Disorders: Psychotherapeutic Strategies*)

Puddu points out that in the contrasting Kohutian model, primacy is accorded to the importance that a well-ordered and cohesive sense of self plays in the developmental process (Puddu, 1999). In the Kohutian world, self-objects play a vital role in ensuring the integrity and psychological health of the self. Self-objects are, simply, other people who have a profound impact on our sense of self, such as one's parents. Kealy and Ogrudniczuk (2014) beautifully describe the function of self-object experiences, telling us that there are two critical kinds of self-object experiences: mirroring and idealizing. Mirroring experiences "confirm the child's greatness and vitality" as a child experiences his/her parents' spontaneous appreciation of the gifts that the child has to offer. Idealizing experiences permit the child "to identify and merge with parents who are calm, effective, and reliable." In this manner, idealizing experiences facilitate internalization of ideals, values, and a mode of being that the child can aspire to. Both mirroring and idealizing experiences "contribute to the development of ambitions and ideals" – or, if one likes, the potentialities that they see in themselves that they can now aspire to and have some hope of fulfilling. The authors write that, together with a range of empathic responses, these self-object relations provide the individual with a sense of strength and vitality with which to pursue their desires and maintain or modify their values in the face of life's challenges. An individual with positive self-object experiences can feel loved, can realistically appraise his or her own ability, and is in a better position to genuinely love others, giving them what he or she has received themselves. "Under optimal conditions, early self-object experiences are (also) provided by parents through their natural empathic responsiveness toward the child... Maturation brings different self-object needs, and therefore different responses from a self-object" (Kealy & Ogrudniczuk, 2014, p. 114). Maturation of the self, in other words, is seen to unfold over the course of a lifetime, reflecting the need of the self to expand and grow, fulfilling aspirational wishes that derive from an appreciation of the self's value.

Teicholz (1978) comments that in a Kohutian world, "narcissistic maturation could be said to represent the story of the gradual accept-ance of the limitations and the goodness, greatness, and power of the self and the parental objects" (Teicholz, 1978, p. 841 citing Kohut (1971) in his book). Mollon helpfully comments that within a Kohut-ian perspective, "the infant is understood as both psychologically sepa-rate and at the same time partially merged with self-object – an idea which is expressed in the notion of two separate lines of development of narcissism (merger with self-object) and object love (relatedness to separate objects)" (Mollon, 1986, p. 156). Stated in another way, Kohut is telling us that love for other people and self-love/self-esteem (which he conceives as deriving from merger with other people who help us appreciate who we are, who we want to be, and why we're lov-able) are two distinct psychological functions. Please keep in mind that "objects" awkwardly and confusingly can refer to both our internal representations of either people and/or our relationships with them, on the one hand, as well as, occasionally, to real people, on the other.

Kealy and Ogrudniczuk (2014) underscore that Kohut accepted the inevitability of empathic breaches as part of anyone's maturational ex-perience. "Repeated, traumatic self object failures, however, (lead) to a fragile self that relies excessively on awkward mechanisms of preserva-tion... (that produce) feelings of deficiency and emptiness" (Kealy & Ogrudniczuk, 2014, p. 115 citing Kohut & Wolf, 1978). In consequence, imposing feelings of shame and a heightened sense of vulnerability to fragmentation of the self in the face of future injury and disappoint-ment could increasingly inform a given individual's experience with themselves. Individuals who carried within them an acute sense of the ease with which they could face personal fragmentation were likely to be very wary in their relationships, hungry for love that might heal them but terribly frightened by the prospect that others would find them deficient, as they did themselves. An acutely fragile fund of resilience would mean that it would be profoundly difficult to expose oneself to potential pain, disappointment, and injury that one could anticipate might feel catastrophic. Even small injuries that could be expected to accumulate during the course of a "normal" relationship could feel too dangerous to try to accommodate in such a personal context.

Unlike Kernberg, who saw grandiosity as the cornerstone upon which the pathological narcissistic self was built, Kohut defined grandiosity as referring either to the self (evident in mirroring transferences in which a patient assumes a grandiose exhibitionistic posture as a means of compelling praise and applause) or to the other (idealizing transferences in which the therapist is idealized) (Bernardi & Eidlin, 2018 referring to Kohut's (1971) book). Besides assuming mirroring and idealizing forms, narcissistic transferences within Kohutian therapy could also demonstrate themselves as twinships, states in which the patient conveyed his sense that he and the therapist were the same. So long as patients demonstrated the three forms of transference just described, the quality of their cathexes or their attachments/relationships to other people could be described as narcissistic. Smith (1988) says of Kohut that it was not the object of cathexis (i.e., the grandiose pathological self), but the quality of cathexis (the form that a relationship assumed) that defined narcissism. Such transferences were attempts to heal the self, to divest the self of its archaic "infantile, imperious, and sadistic quality" (Mollon, 1986, p. 155). Puddu (1999) described the healing process in Kohutian therapy as an attempt to repair the ruptures in self-development that inadequate self-object relations created for it, searching for healing experiences that the analyst can provide through attunement to introspection and empathy. From this perspective, Kohut could be seen to direct much of his focus on narcissism as a form of arrested development that denied patients the opportunity to appropriately value themselves and others, while Kernberg, in contrast, focused on the destructive aspects of the grandiose self. Also unlike Kernberg, Kohut thought the disturbances in the formation of the self – which he viewed as structuralized into a grandiose pole (a repository for ambition), an idealizing pole (a repository for internalized ideals), and a tension arc between the two – assumed greater importance than the impact of object relations (Mollon, 1986).

During the third and final stage of Kohut's work, Kohut was said to move away from self-psychology as a complementary framework toward one in which it established its centrality:

> Self psychology is now attempting to demonstrate... that all forms of psychopathology are based either on deficits in the structure of the self, on distortions of the self, or on weakness of the self. It is

trying to show, furthermore, that all these flaws in the self are due to disturbances of self-object relationships in childhood. Stated in the obverse by way of highlighting the contrast between self psychological and traditional theory, self psychology holds that pathogenic conflicts in the object instinctual realm – that is pathogenic conflicts in the realm of object love and hate… are not the primary cause of psychopathology, but its result.

(Mollon, 1986, p. 53)

Parenthetically, Kohut actually softened his position some pages later in *How Does Analysis Cure* (1984), which is where the Mollon quote comes from:

By listening open mindedly, I mean that (the analyst) must resist the temptation to squeeze his understanding of the patient into the rigid mold of whatever theoretical preconception he may hold, be they Kleinian, Rankian, Jungian, Adlerian, classical analytic, or, yes, self psychological… (p. 67)

Later in his third book he adds:

… they become concrete entities, demanding that we force the data we observe in the rubric of an unalterable scheme. My own attitude toward the classifications I have proposed has always been that they are temporary, changeable, improvable – in short, that they will cease to be useful if we are unwilling to alter them in order to accommodate new insights or facts. (p. 203)

Kernberg (1991), in contrast, found it hard to conceive that a self and/or ego could predate what he considered to be the first foundational experiences of a child's life, which were reflected in its interaction with others. In this sense, he was very much in agreement with Melanie Klein's object relations position, which insisted that the evolution of a child's important internal structures derived from the representations of their encounters with other people that they constructed inside themselves.

The distinction between the two positions is challenging to grasp. Kohut would say that mirroring and idealizing experiences with parents allowed the child to construct the all-important sense of self upon which all other psychological structures rested. Kernberg believed that a child's internal representations of his/her relationships with others eventually allowed the child to build an ego and a self. Debate about the evolution of the self and what a self is has been a preoccupation within psychoanalytic theory as psychoanalytic ideas have developed and refined themselves over the years. The evolving discourse about self is certainly an example of why a foundational concept like narcissism, which implicates conceptions of self, remains so difficult to grasp. More will be said about self in a later section of this book.

In reflecting upon the relative advantages and disadvantages of self-psychology, Mollon (1986) suggested that focus on the concept of the self and its subjectivity had allowed us to more effectively articulate our own phenomenology, that greater understanding of affects like joy was possible, and that Kohut had successfully identified three important forms of transference phenomena. He also cautioned that Kohut failed to pay full accord to the dark forces in our nature, that Kohut's approach may foster a naïve disregard that the images of figures the patient experiences as unempathetic could be infused with the patient's own destructive impulses, and that, in addition to mirroring and idealizing experiences with parents, a child required a parent to understand their emotional experiences in an intimate way that could be reflected back to the child in terms that the child could understand and appreciate.

Hinze echoed some of Mollon's concerns, reflecting that "the intricate relationship between narcissism and object relations is not appreciated enough, and the role of aggression and destructive impulses in the human mind is minimized" (Hinze, 2017, p. 27). At the same time, she felt that Kohut's approach had furthered "a more permissive, truly analytic attitude toward narcissistic phenomena…" (Hinze, 2017, p. 27). My own sense, as I discussed in my previous book, *A Study of Malignant Narcissism*, is that Kohut only brushed up against some of the more destructive forms of narcissism (which I refer to as malignant narcissism), but, interestingly, his framing of this form of narcissism is very similar to Kernberg's. Berke (1985) reminds us that Kohut did appreciate the relationship between narcissism and envy: "… Chronic narcissistic rage (is) one of the most pernicious afflictions of the human psyche – either in its still endogenous and preliminary form, as a grudge and spite; or, externalized and acted out, to disconnected vengeful acts or to cunningly plotted vendettas" (Kohut, 1972, pp. 396–397). Kohut has also been criticized by others for suggesting that empathy is enough to lead to healing. I cited his impassioned response to this criticism in my original book, a response in which he reiterates the importance he placed upon interpretation as a central focal point of any therapeutic endeavor.

So how do we accommodate ourselves to two such seemingly contrasting and, in some ways, opposing theoretical positions in which differences loom larger than similarities? Do we accept the Kernbergian view that narcissism is built around a pathological self marked by grandiosity, aggression, and resistance to reflection, producing an intense, up-and-down countertransference experience for the therapist who is expected to actively attack the patient's destructiveness – or do we embrace Kohut's view of the patient as trying to heal himself and as seeking out mirroring, idealizing, and twinship encounters with an empathic, accepting therapist in order to do so? In the Kernbergian model, focus is placed on an intransigent, antagonistic self that is determined – almost at all costs – to hang onto its grandiosity, while for Kohut, the patient is conceived as experiencing painful subjective deficiency and vulnerability that make it hard for him or her to function in the world.

Shane (2014) offers us one answer. She asks whether the differences in the two theoretical positions might have arisen because Kohut and Kernberg used different groups of patients to build their models upon. Ornstein (1974) raised a similar question, wondering whether Kernberg and Kohut were "even talking about the same patient population and that perhaps, with the exception of the more severely disturbed of Kohut's patient population, they indeed are not" (cited in Teicholz, 1978, p. 857). Our discussion in Chapter 2 about grandiose or thick-skinned narcissism versus vulnerable or thin-skinned narcissism may have a further bearing on the differences that we see between these two important practitioners.

Kohut (1984) also raised another very important question, at least in my estimate: do the theoretical frameworks that we construct to guide us also significantly impact what we see and what we don't see? In *The Restoration of the Self*, he notes that:

> The theories held by the observer influence not only what he sees – in our case, what he sees when he scrutinizes the psychoanalytic process and its results – (but also) how he evaluates what he sees, what he deems to be central and significant, and what he dismisses as peripheral, insignificant, or trite. (p. 41)

To my mind, this is what any scientific endeavor is like. It means that it is incumbent upon each of us to grapple with the entanglements other people refer to as narcissism, bringing our own experience and discernment to the work that needs to be done, perhaps, in the process, adding to the cacophony, but in the longer run serving to bring us closer to understanding the mysteries of what it means to be human. There has indeed been progress – significant progress – yielding new knowledge and new conceptualizations that vastly advantage us compared to those early practitioners who tried so hard to make sense of what narcissism was.

I very much agree with Mollon (1986) that "mental development is too complex to be adequately accommodated within any one psychoanalytic model" (p. 160). While he was referring to Kohut's wish to establish his model as a standalone model of psychodynamics that was sufficient unto itself, I think his comments remind us that we all need each other and each other's ideas/theoretical constructions to at least partially grasp, in a given instance, what we're seeing in our diagnostic and therapeutic work with the people who come to us for help. As can be seen from Kohut's own appraisal of his theoretical formulations, he was very much aware of their limitations, notwithstanding the seeming conviction that attended his view of their centrality.

In formulating my own ideas about malignant narcissism, I relied heavily upon other theorists, including Fromm, Kernberg, Mika, Hughes, Kohut, and Shaw, among a number of others. Each theorist and each voice had his or her own gifts to offer, and all of these "gifts" were essential to me in my personal journey to piece together an understanding of what malignant narcissism is. With specific reference to Kohut and to Kernberg, Kohut's concept of "self" proved essential to me, providing me with the cornerstone upon which I could base my work, as did Kernberg's appreciation of the grandiose self and his evocative description of the inner world of someone struggling with NPD, pervaded, as it appears to be, by an accumulation of all of the dark objects that have piled up inside over the course of a lifetime. Both theorists emphasized the risks that fragmentation poses for the narcissistic self, though from different perspectives. Both theorists (much like Fromm) called our attention to the harm that extreme forms of narcissism can pose for the human community as well as articulating some of the dynamics of narcissistic group regression. The foregoing, of course, encompasses only a small part of the numerous insights these two men have bequeathed us. In mentioning some of the more prominent (for me) contributions that each made to my work, I hope to underscore how interdependent we are upon one another to construct new vistas of understanding.

In order to take advantage of others' insights, then, I had to stand away from doctrinaire adherence to a particular school of thought, applying ideas flexibly and hopefully creatively in a fashion that best seemed to suit the material I was working with. I do want to mention, however, that the efforts that Kernberg and his associates at Weill Cornell have undertaken over decades probably represent the most organized, extensive, systematic study of narcissism that is currently available to any of us. It is truly impressive work that is very ably summarized in their new book, *Treating Pathological Narcissism*, published in 2022.

The current book will draw extensively upon a variety of points of view and schools of psychoanalytic thought. My intention is to offer readers necessarily limited portraits of some of the most salient theoretical conceptions or part conceptions that we have available to us currently. I will apologize, at the outset, that I won't have the space to include many of the theorists whom I could mention and who undoubtedly deserve to be mentioned.

I hope to continue the discussion of narcissism that I have initiated by focusing on our evolving understanding of the processes that underlie grandiose or thick-skinned narcissism versus vulnerable or thin-skinned narcissism.

References

Auerbach, J. (1990). Narcissism. *Psychoanalytic Psychology*, *7*(4), 545–564.

Berke, J. (1985). Envy loveth not: A study of the origin, influence and the confluence of envy and narcissism. *British Journal of Psychotherapy*, *1*(3), 171–186.

Bernardi, R., & Eidlin, M. (2018). Thin-skinned or vulnerable narcissism and thick-skinned or grandiose narcissism: Similarities and differences. *International Journal of Psychoanalysis*, *99*(2), 291–313.

Britton, R. (2004). Narcissistic disorders in clinical practice. *Journal of Analytical Psychology*, *49*, 477–490.

Diamond, D., Yeomans, F. E., Stern, B. L., & Kernberg O. F. (2022). *Treating pathological narcissism with transference-focused psychotherapy*. The Guilford Press.

Hinze, E. (2017). Narcissism: Is it still a useful psychoanalytic concept? *Romanian Journal of Psychoanalysis*, *10*(2), 19–34.

Jones, E. (1955). *The life and work of Sigmund Freud. Vol. II Years of Maturity, 1901–1919*. Hogarth Press.

Kealy, D., & Ogrudniczuk, J. (2014). Pathological narcisisism and the obstruction of love. *Psychodynamic Psychiatry*, *42*(1), 101–119.

Kernberg, O. (1970). Factors in the treatment of narcissistic personalities. *Journal of the American Psychoanalytic Association*, *18*, 51–85.

Kernberg, O. (1984). *Severe personality disorders*. Yale University Press.

Kernberg, O. (1991). A contemporary reading of narcissism. In J. Sandler, E. S. Person, & P. Fonagy (Eds.), *Freud on narcissism: An introduction* (pp. 131–148). Yale University Press.

Kohut, H. (1971). *The analysis of the self*. International University Press.

Kohut, H. (1972). Thoughts on narcissism and narcissistic rage. *Psychoanalytic Study of the Child*, *27*, 360–400.

Kohut, H., & Wolf, E. S. (1978). The disorders of the self and their treatment: An outline. *International Journal of Psychoanalysis*, *59*, 413–425.

Kohut, H. (1984). *How does analysis cure?* University of Chicago Press.

Lester, L. (2000). Normal and pathological narcissism in women. Changing Ideas in a Changing World: The Revolution in Psychoanalysis: Essays in Honour of Arnold Cooper, (38):87–93.

Meissner, S. J. (2008). Narcissism and the self: Psychoanalytic considerations. *The Journal of the American Academy of Psychoanalysis and Dynamic Psychiatry*, *36*(3), 461–494.

Mollon, P. (1986). An appraisal of Kohut's contribution to the understanding of narcissism. *British Journal of Psychotherapy*, *3*(2), 151–161.

Moore, B. F. (1975). Toward a clarification of the concept of narcissism. *Psychoanalytic Study of the Child*, *30*, 243–276.

Ornstein, P. H. (1974). A discussion of the paper by Otto Kernberg on "Further contributions to the treatment of narcissistic personalities." *International Journal of Psychoanalysis*, *55*, 241–247.

Puddu, R. (1999). Discussion of the Petri Meronen paper, the return of narcissism. *International Forum of Psychoanalysis*, *8*(3–4), 221–226.

Pulver, S. E. (1970). Narcissism: The term and concept. *Journal of the American Psychoanalytic Association*, (18):319–341. Eliminate American St. Child 30.

Shane, E. (2014). The generation of the romantic ideal by a self-disordered patient. *Psychoanalytic Inquiry*, *34*(5), 430–439.

Shaw, D. (2013). *Traumatic narcissism: Relational systems of subjugation*. Routledge.

Smith, D. (1988). Narcissism since Freud: Towards a unified theory. *British Journal of Psychotherapy*, *4*(3), 302–312.

Stolorow, R. D. (1975). The narcissistic function of masochism (and sadism). *The International Journal of Psychoanalysis*, *56*, 441–448.

Taylor, C. (1992). *The ethics of authenticity*. Harvard University Press.

Teicholz, J. (1978). A selective review of psychoanalytic literature on theoretical conceptualizations of narcissism. *Journal of the American Psychoanalytic Association*, *26*, 831–861.

Chapter 2

Thick-Skinned or Grandiose Narcissism (GN) and Thin-Skinned or Vulnerable Narcissism (VN)

The next topic to be discussed extends our focus on the confusion which has attended conceptualizations of pathological narcissism. It also draws us into an exploration of major contemporary trends in our thinking that define our understanding of narcissism.

Bernardi and Eidlin (2018) remind us that the two forms of narcissism being referenced have been given a variety of different names by different theorists: thin or thick-skinned narcissism (Rosenfeld, 1987a; Kernberg, 2014); grandiose versus vulnerable narcissism (VN) (Akhtar & Thompson, 1982; Caligor et al., 2015; Cooper & Ronningstam, 1982; Dickinson & Pincus, 2003); indifferent or oblivious narcissism and hypervigilant narcissism (Gabbard, 1989); hyper subjective and hyper objective narcissism (Britton, 1989); and arrogant, open, grandiose, assertive, aggressive narcissism and shy, covert, vulnerable, shame driven narcissism (Ronningstam, 2009). To this list, Diamond et al. (2022) add overt and covert (Cooper, 1998) and arrogant/entitled and depressed/depleted or manipulative and phallic versus craving and paranoid (Burstein, 1973), prompting us to remember that Cain et al. (2008) cataloged over 50 different labels distinguishing between the two prominent phenotypic expressions of narcissism. It naturally far exceeds the purview of this book to critically review each of these conceptions; rather, I chronicle them so that the reader has a sense that a significant number of authors recognize two characteristic, prominent forms of narcissism whose delineations many theorists can more or less agree upon.

So – in broad terms – how have these two forms of narcissism been characterized? Thick-skinned or grandiose narcissism (GN) is generally recognized as that form of narcissism that rests upon a pathological or grandiose self-structure. Its prominent characteristics most closely

DOI: 10.4324/9781032649535-2

align themselves with Diagnostic and Statistical Manual-5 (DSM-5) descriptions of Narcissistic Personality Disorder (NPD). DSM-5 focuses on providing a symptomatic portrait of any given personality disorder, eschewing descriptions of relevant psychodynamics in contrast to the Psychodynamic Diagnostic Manual (PDM-2), which establishes categorizations on the basis of dynamics. The symptom cluster attributed to NPD includes, as at least a partial list, a pervasive pattern of grandiosity, need for admiration, lack of empathy, preoccupation with fantasies of unlimited success, a sense of entitlement, preoccupation with envy, and arrogant, haughty behaviors or attitudes. Bernardi and Eidlin (2018), citing Rosenfeld (1987b), tell us that such personalities are oblivious to profound feelings, inaccessible, and characterized by intense envy that leads to a devaluation of the analyst and analysis, as well as any dependency situation. Diamond et al. (2022) characterize grandiose or thick-skinned presentation as being typified by "an exaggerated sense of self-importance, striving for social dominance and exploitation of others to attain it, and a sense of entitlement rage when it is threatened or challenged" (p. 24). They also add that "these are all the overt manifestations of more covert cognitions, such as fantasies of unlimited success" (p. 24).

My own work with malignant narcissism and my clinical work with NPD in my practice would place emphasis upon thick-skinned or GN – as an abbreviated description – as a state in which profound, intransigent mistrust of others occasioned by early relational trauma has come to mean that it is too dangerous to allow oneself to need others or to lean on them, or even love them or be loved by them; that the self creates protection for itself by investing in a solipsistic existence defined by a sense of grandiosity and omnipotence, by its refusal to authenticate other voices (save as a means to exploit them), and by erecting walls of contempt, hostility, arrogance, and haughtiness as a means of ensuring that meaningful interconnection with other people can never be realized. I also believe that the inability to love or be loved produces, as Kernberg has suggested in his description of the inner world of the narcissist, an emaciated, envious, paranoid interior that offers little sustenance while provoking intense oral rage and acquisitiveness (Wood, 2023). For clarity, I am describing forms of GN in which narcissistic pathology is particularly prominent.

It is important to keep in mind, as Kernberg does (previously described), that grandiose or thick-skinned narcissism may be typified by significant differences in the level at which a given personality functions, producing, in the process, a more or a less deleterious clinical picture and life experience. As previously mentioned, many significant aspects of my conception of pathological narcissism and malignant narcissism in particular rest on the shoulders of the work many other clinicians have done.

Thin-skinned or VN, very much in contrast, is described by Bernardi and Eidlin (2018) as being pervaded by "painful internal experiences of vulnerability, inferiority, emptiness, boredom, fear, and lack of self-confidence" (p. 293). Diamond et al. (2022) portray a vulnerable or thin-skinned presentation as being informed by "hypersensitivity to rejection, a sense of unworthiness, and feelings of inadequacy in the context of covert grandiose features evident primarily in fantasies, beliefs, and entitled expectations, the behavioural expression of which is curtailed by inhibition, self effacement, and shame proneness" (p. 24 referencing the work of Kernberg (1984) and Cain et al. (2008)). Later, they comment that shame and a profound sense of inferiority prompt a "retreat to a grandiose illusory world that insulates them from others, from the limitations in the self, and even in more extreme cases from aspects of reality itself" (p. 61). The gap between the aspirations that their grandiose expectations of self generate versus the disappointing actualities of their life propels them to withdraw from others. In the case of thin-skinned narcissism, grandiosity and entitlement are hidden and covert, in other words, but nevertheless play a central role in the way that the thin-skinned narcissist is organized.

Numbers of clinicians argue that what we are seeing is a broad variation in the phenotypic expression of narcissism, effectively maintaining that grandiose and thick-skinned narcissism (GN sometimes called NG) versus vulnerable/thin-skinned narcissism (VN sometimes called NV) are potentially two faces of the same disorder (see, e.g., Fossati et al., 2015, among numerous others). Diamond et al. (2022) assert that "there is now a consensus that those with pathological narcissism may have quite varied presentations, the most typical of which are grandiose or thick-skinned or vulnerable or thin-skinned" (citing Bateman, 1998; Rosenfeld, 1971, 1987a). Later, they state that "each narcissistic patient is often a unique admixture of grandiosity and vulnerability. In individuals with pathological narcissism, one state may be more prominent than others, but they will usually oscillate between grandiosity and vulnerability over the course of treatment…" (p. 62). Elsewhere, they add that patients rated higher on vulnerability tend to show greater fluctuation between grandiosity and vulnerability than patients rated higher on grandiosity (see Edershile & Wright, 2019).

Diamond et al. (2022) identify exploitativeness, self-centeredness, entitlement, and interpersonal antagonism as "core personality features" of both of the two faces of narcissism. Certainly, these features stand out clearly with GN, being less obvious manifestations of VN. Clinical examples that they provide portray vulnerable narcissists as being perpetually preoccupied with their need to protect themselves from the emotional buffeting that others can create for them through criticism or judgment as they struggle with covert grandiose expectations that they live with internally. Diamond et al. (2022) state that "they may annex themselves to others whom they perceive as special and/or worthy of admiration that they themselves crave but cannot attain… (Sometimes) ceaselessly unload(ing) experiences of maltreatment or self-loathing in the form of rigid or fixed narratives that make them feel special and unique…" (pp. 64–65). In an earlier passage, they refer to the vulnerable narcissist's inclination to establish special status for themselves "through glorification of their distress and suffering" (p. 61). In still another passage, referencing Akhtar (2009), they suggest that vulnerable narcissists "react to threats to self-esteem or (to an) unrealistically inflated self-image not with aggression or animosity, but with withdrawal, contemptuous dismissal, or attempts to control others" (p. 64).

For me, this is the weakest part of the argument to be made for the similarity between the two states; what I think I'm hearing is not exploitativeness, self-centeredness, entitlement, and interpersonal antagonism so much as someone for whom trauma has created a great deal of pain and a profound sense of fragility that renders it quite challenging for them to navigate their way through the world of people in a manner that would feel safe for them. Phrases like "glorification of their distress" and "ceaselessly unload experiences of maltreatment and self-loathing" strike me as gratuitously pejorative and ill-suited to an analytic context. I do, however, see that VN likely incorporates grandiose elements. I am also in partial agreement that both purported forms of narcissism are associated with a sense of fragility of the self (Caligor et al., 2015), but I would add that the experience of fragility is different in GN versus VN, the former being characterized by a poorly recognized sense of precariousness that attend the business of keeping one's grandiosity afloat while the latter instigates profound, painful subjective awareness of the self's instability. Bernardi and Eidlin (2018) also consider that both forms manifest difficulties in getting along with others and that both rely on others to confirm their self-esteem.

It strikes me, however, that the differences in the way that they relate to other people and the quality of concern that each has about their self-esteem are sufficiently different that any attempt to identify similarities feels more contrived than substantive.

In what I believe to be an important passage, Fossati et al. (2015) cite Pincus and Lukowitsky's conclusion that what may differentiate narcissistic patients from one another is their relative levels of grandiosity and vulnerability. The clinical examples of GN and VN provided in the literature do very much attest to the combination of both elements in narcissistic patients with patients demonstrating oscillation between one state and the other, but, again, I see important qualitative differences that divide patients who are predominantly GN versus patients who are predominantly VN. The line that distinguishes patients who are predominantly GN or predominantly VN is admittedly sometimes difficult to appreciate, but it is a distinction I would argue is a critical one that attests to important qualitative differences between the two predominant positions and, as such, is essential to keep in mind in our work with people.

I will talk further about the viability of regarding both GN and VN as different faces of narcissism much later in this discussion when I reflect upon my own clinical work and that of Daniel Shaw. For the moment and for ease of discussion, let's accept that both GN and VN are, in fact, different forms of narcissism. I'd like now to review some literature that's pertinent to these forms.

Kernberg (1975) and Ronningstam (2005) have suggested that GN patients may be relatively free of subjective imbalance (referring to declarative experiences of personal distress) unless they encounter significant life reversals or interpersonal failures (referenced by Bernardi & Eidlin, 2018). Research that Miller et al. (2007) conducted led them to conclude that GNs functioning at higher levels not only reported less subjective distress but were likely to create higher levels of distress in others. Bernardi and Eidlin cite Hibbert's 1992 work suggesting that a propensity for shame is statistically related to VN but not GN. Hibbert's work further suggested that a successful narcissistic defense (referring to GN) shuts down shame experiences through solicitation of praise from others. Several authors (Miller & Campbell, 2008; Pincus & Lukowitsky, 2010; Russ et al., 2008) concluded that depression, anxiety, non-suicidal self-injury, and suicide attempts were commonly observed in VN patients (see Bernardi and Eidlin again). Bateman's work (1998) suggested that movement between VN and GN states increases the likelihood of aggression toward others when GN predominates and aggression toward the self when VN does. Pincus et al. (2009) found that VN patients were more inclined to seek out treatment for themselves, concluding that clinicians were more likely to see narcissistic patients when they were in a vulnerable self-state. Ellison et al. (2013) also found that relatively higher levels of VN appear to contribute to higher levels of subjective distress that impel patients to seek treatment (see Fossati et al., 2015). Rosenfeld (1971) cautioned that such patients dismissed or stonewalled depth work, protecting a rigid, fixed, and unyielding narrative that could contribute to a sense of impotence in the therapist (cited in Diamond et al., 2022).

Fossati et al. argued that VN implicates impaired self-regulatory functions reflected in experiences of anger, envy, aggression, helplessness, emptiness, low self-esteem, shame, social avoidance, and even suicidality" (citing Pincus et al., 2015). Pincus et al. (2014) suggested that such depression is characterized more by feelings of emptiness, uselessness, and suicidal ideation than it is by grief and sadness. In reviewing this study, Bernardi and Eidlin (2018) commented that in response to depression of this type, patients seek help, feel afraid of being let down, are ashamed of needing others, and are likely subject to outbursts of rage and outbursts of hostility, culminating in depression and more shame when their demands for recognition are not met. Later in their paper, Fossati et al. reference a number of research studies (Dickinson & Pincus, 2003; Otway & Vignoles, 2006; Smolewska & Dion, 2005) that suggest GN is "characterized by a sense of confidence in self and others in both clinical and nonclinical samples, suggesting that GN may play a self-protective role, creating an idealized 'safe haven' for pathological narcissists" (p. 423). Such research makes good intuitive sense: people in significant distress struggling with imposing symptomatology (VN) are more likely to feel the need to ameliorate their suffering than someone who can turn away or significantly mitigate their pain by investing themselves in a predominantly grandiose posture (GN). The further implication of this research is that as narcissistic people vacillate between VN and GN, they are most likely to solicit psychotherapy intervention when they are in a VN state.

Fossati et al. cautioned that while "VN may motivate narcissistic clients to seek treatment, it is strongly connected with attachment insecurities involving opposite strategies. In VN, the narcissistic client is conflicted over deep fears related to the lack of a secure base and the illusion (that a sense of security) can be restored by dismissing caregiving relationships. In contrast, GN involves a sense of security based on an unrealistic sense of self-worth and pretended autonomy; clinical consideration suggests that GN may be involved in unilateral treatment terminations" (p. 424). In the study that the Fossati group undertook exploring the relationship between attachment styles and NPD, they concluded that VN "seemed to involve a complex interplay of painful perception of dependency needs leading to over activation of the attachment system (i.e., anxious attachment; Mikulincer & Shaver, 2007) and an attempt at deactivating the attachment system by displacing dependency needs from human relationships to money, power, status, and so forth... (with) no achieved sense of security" (p. 423). When people with NPD were defined by VN, in other words, they alternated between pushing people away and dismissing them, on the one hand, and anxiously soliciting their attention and support, on the other. In considering the relationship between attachment strategies and NPD, Fossati et al. referenced the work of Zeigler-Hill et al. (2011), which suggested that both GN and VN were positively correlated with concern about mistrust and abandonment, "reflecting beliefs that others will abuse, manipulate, or leave them" (p. 423). The Ziegler-Hill research was also said to suggest that people with GN held the belief that the self was perfect and that it was entitled to have whatever it wanted, whereas VN seemed to entail a belief "in unrealistically high standards in a world of important others where emotional expression and interpersonal dependency have negative consequences" (p. 424).

As the Fossati group considered the relationship between attachment styles and NPD, they commented that: "... Our negative finding is in line with the lack of consistent associations between NPD and insecure attachment that have been reported by the majority of studies..." (p. 422). Later in their article, they conclude that "one developmental model might not be able to account for all the variants of pathological narcissism and attachment" (p. 423). Nonetheless, the suggestion that people who are either predominantly VN or struggling with a shift into a VN state fluctuate between anxiety about their attachments and a need to dismiss or deny the importance of their attachments is, for me, a compelling perspective. It also strikes me that the complex interplay of attachment styles within VN renders identification of an overall attachment style for NPD rather challenging.

Skodel et al. (2015) pointed out that including vulnerable forms of narcissism meant that one would now also be embracing narcissistic disorders characterized by a neurotic level of organization. In contrast,

Akhtar and Thompson's work in 1982, cited in Bernardi and Eidlin, suggested to them that while narcissistic disorders shared both impaired capacity for empathy and reliance on the defense of splitting with people functioning at the borderline level, narcissistic disorders also enjoyed greater cohesion of the self, impulse control, containment of aggression, and stability of reality testing. They went on to caution that their conception of narcissistic disorders functioning at a higher level than borderline disorders may be especially true of the grandiose forms of narcissism. Other researchers (Di Piero et al., 2019) also drew similar conclusions, characterizing VN as demonstrating greater identity diffusion and personality organization more likely to fall in the borderline realm. The Diamond group commented that "for thick-skinned individuals, defences are more rigid and effective in shoring up the grandiosity and establishing a beachhead of dominance and supremacy that keeps devalued aspects of the self (at bay)" (p. 62). A bit later they elaborate: "higher functioning narcissistic individuals are likely to be more grandiose and thick-skinned… However, the two presentations of narcissistic pathology may characterize those at all levels of personality organization" (referencing Rosenfeld, 1971). At another point in their review of research findings about GN and VN, they also called attention to comments that Rosenfeld (1971) and others have made about people whose orientation was primarily VN, saying of them that even though they might seem to have transcended much of their suffering and their extraordinary challenges, appearing to have established satisfactory adjustments in their work and love lives, they could often be expected to demonstrate chronically self-defeating behaviors and even extreme self-destructiveness. The import of such appraisals is a kind of inescapable spiritual destitution one could expect to dog the steps of a VN orientation.

Notwithstanding the stickiness, Diamond et al. (2022) describe between level of function and phenotypic expression of narcissism; they concluded, "we might say that grandiose/thick-skinned and vulnerable/thin-skinned presentation is a dimension that is orthogonal to the level of personality organization…" (p. 62) Importantly, they also cautioned that "… as clinicians we encounter a number of patients in whom pathological narcissism comingles with other characterological features that lead to more complex finely grained and varied presentations…" (p. 62). Later, they emphasized that "there are few overarching theories that would explain why those with pathological narcissism may have such variable presentations and why these dimensions of narcissistic disorder may coexist within the same individual" (p. 70). Helpfully, they called for more in-depth research that might enable them to better delineate the relationship between GN and VN oscillations in relation to a variety of other variables such as shifts in self-esteem, affect regulation, interpersonal functioning, and overall level of personality organization, as examples.

Before turning toward an examination of clinical examples of GN and VN, let's revisit the question, were Kohut and Kernberg looking at the same groups of patients? Consider, now, how Kohut described patients he identified as narcissistic in his first book, *The Analysis of the Self* (1974):

> ... Vague complaints about depressed mood, lack of zest and initiative in the area of work, dullness of interpersonal experience, the patient's uneasiness about his physical or mental state, multiple perverse trends, and the like, will point toward the area of narcissistic disturbance... Behind a vague complaint about lack of initiative or zest the analyst... will discover the presence of diffuse narcissistic vulnerability, of circumscribed defects in self-esteem or self-esteem regulation, or broad disturbances in the patient's system of ideals.... (p. 22)

Other comments that he made in the context of the same discussion emphasized narcissistic personality's vulnerability to disapproval, shame, object loss, and the ideals that others could impose that could occasion distress. The portrait that emerged was of a personality that was utterly dependent upon others' appraisal, was ill-equipped to support its own self-esteem, and probably struggled with underlying, grandiose ideals which represented a source of suffering and, possibly, envy.

Sounds an awful lot like VN, doesn't it?

In interesting adjacent passage he comments that:

> in those cases where the psychopathology of the narcissistic personality is expressed in more circumscribed and colorful syndromes... the patient may voice the following complaints and present the following pathological features: (1) in the sexual sphere: perverse fantasies, lack of interest in sex; (2) the social sphere: work inhibitions, inability to form and maintain significant relationships, delinquent activities; (3) in his manifest personality features: lack of humor,

lack of empathy for other people's needs and feelings, lack of sense of proportion, tendency towards attacks of uncontrolled rage, pathological lying; and (4) in the psychosomatic sphere: hypochondriacal preoccupations with physical and mental health, vegetative disturbances in various organ systems. (p. 23)

The "colorful syndromes" he appears to be referencing sound closer to GN, don't they? He describes grandiosity as the state "in which the child attempts to save the originally all-embracing narcissism by concentrating perfection and power upon the self – here called the grandiose self – and by turning away disdainfully from an outside to which all imperfections have been assigned" (p. 106). Such a description sounds very Kernbergian. In a still later passage, however, he says:

Ominous as the manifestations of these regressive states would seem to be, in most instances neither analyst nor patient become unduly alarmed by them. There are rare exceptions, it is true…; But in the vast majority of the cases of the type of pathology with which this study is concerned these regressions are clearly a part of the therapeutic process and are soon accepted by the patient as grist for the mill of the insight producing work which leads to the gradual expansion and strengthening of his ego. (pp. 136–137)

Now it would seem that the grandiosity that Kohut refers to in his "colorful syndromes" is relatively transient after all, not the enduring, defining state that would, for instance, typify predominant GN. These comments invite one to think – once again – that the group patients which Kohut references in his writing are predominantly VN, not GN, in contrast to Kernberg's foundational conceptions of narcissism that would seem to extend from a patient group that sounded to be substantially more GN than VN. Please keep in mind that I regard these ideas as propositional.

References

Akhtar, S. (2009). Love, sex and marriage in the setting of pathological narcissism. *Psychiatric Annals*, *39*(4), 185–191.

Akhtar, S., & Thompson, J. J. (1982). Overview: Narcissistic personality disorder. *American Journal of Psychiatry*, *139*(1), 12–20.

Bateman, A. (1998). Thick- and thin-skinned organizations and enactment in borderline and narcissistic disorders. *International Journal of Psychoanalysis*, *79*(Pt. 1), 13–25.

Bernardi, R., & Eidlin, M. (2018). Thin-skinned or vulnerable narcissism and thick-skinned or grandiose narcissism: Similarities and differences. *International Journal of Psychoanalysis*, *99*(2), 291–313.

Britton, R. (1989). The missing link: Parental sensitivity in the Oedipus complex. In Steiner, J. (Ed.) *Today clinical implications* (pp. 83–101). Karnac Books.

Burstein, B. (1973). Some narcissistic personality types. *International Journal of Psychoanalysis*, *54*(3), 287–300.

Cain, N. M., Pincus, A. L., & Ansell, E. B. (2008). Narcissism at the crossroads: Phenotypic description of pathological narcissism across clinical theory, social/personality psychology, and psychiatric diagnosis. *Clinical Psychology Review*, *28*(4), 638–656.

Caligor, E., Levy, K. N., & Yeomans, F. E. (2015). Narcissistic personality disorder: Diagnostic and clinical challenges. *American Journal of Psychiatry*, *172*(5), 415–422.

Cooper, A. M. (1998). Further developments in the clinical diagnosis of narcissistic personality disorder. In E. F. Ronningstam (Ed.), *Disorders of narcissism: Diagnostic, clinical, and empirical implications* (pp. 53–74). American Psychiatric Press.

Cooper, A. M., & Ronningstam, E. (1982). Narcissistic personality disorder. *Review of Psychiatry*, *11*(5), 80–98.

Diamond, D., Yeomans, F. E., Stern, B. L., & Kernberg O. F. (2022). *Treating pathological narcissism with transference-focused psychotherapy*. The Guilford Press.

Dickinson, K. A., & Pincus, A. L. (2003). Interpersonal analysis of grandiose and vulnerable narcissism. *Journal of Personality Disorders*, *17*(3), 188–207.

Di Piero, R., Costantini, G., Benzi, I. M., Madeddu, F., & Preti, E. (2019). Grandiose and entitled, but still fragile: A network analysis of pathological narcissistic traits. *Personality and Individual Differences*, *140*, 15–20.

Edershile, E. A., & Wright, A. G. (2019). Grandiose and vulnerable narcissistic states in interpersonal situations. *Self and Identity*, *20*(2), 1–7.

Ellison, W. D. Levy, K. N., Cain, N. M., Ansell, E. B., & Pincus, A. L. (2013). The impact of pathological narcissism on psychotherapy utilization, initial symptom severity, and early treatment symptom change: A naturalistic investigation. *Journal of Personality Assessment*, *95*(3), 291–300.

Fossati, A. Feeney, J., Pincus, A., Borroni, S., & Maffei, C. (2015). The structure of pathological narcissism and its relationships with adult attachment styles. *Psychoanalytic Psychology*, *32*(3), 403–431.

Gabbard, G. O. (1989). Two types of narcissistic personality disorder. *Bulletin of the Menninger Clinic*, *53*, 527–532.

Hibbard, S. (1992). Narcissism, shame, masochism, and object relations: An exploratory correlational study. *Psychoanalytic Psychology, 9,* 489–508.

Kernberg, O. F. (1975). *Borderline conditions and pathological narcissism.* Jason Aronson.

Kernberg, O. F. (1984). *Severe personality disorders: Psychotherapeutic strategies.* Yale University Press.

Kernberg, O. F. (2014). An overview of the treatment of severe narcissistic pathology. *International Journal of Psychoanalysis, 95*(5), 865–888.

Mikulincer, M., & Shaver, P. R. (2007). Reflections on security dynamics: Core constructs, psychological mechanisms, relational contexts, and the need for an integrative theory. *Psychological Inquiry, 18,* 197–209.

Miller, J., & Campbell, W. (2008). Comparing clinical and social-personality conceptualizations of narcissism. *Journal of Personality, 76,* 449–476.

Miller, J. D., Campbell, W. K., & Pilkonis, P. A. (2007). Narcissistic personality disorder: Relations with distress and functional impairment. *Comprehensive Psychiatry, 48*(2), 170–177.

Otway, L. J., & Vignoles, V. L. (2006). Narcissism and childhood recollections: A quantitative test of psychological predictions. *Personality and Social Psychology Bulletin, 32,* 104–116.

Pincus, A. L., Anseell, E. B., Pimental, C. A., Cain, N. M., Wright, A. G. C., & Levy, K. N. (2009). Initial construction and validation of the pathological narcissism inventory. *Psychological Assessment, 21*(3), 365–379.

Pincus, A. L., Cain, N. M., & Wright, A. G. C. (2014). Narcissistic grandiosity and narcissistic vulnerability in psychotherapy. *Personality Disorders: Theory, Research, and Treatment, 5*(4), 439–443.

Pincus, A. L., & Lukowitsky, M. R. (2010). Pathological narcissism and narcissistic personality disorder. *Annual Review of Clinical Psychology, 6,* 421–446.

Pincus, A. L., Roche, M. J., & Good, E. W. (2015). Narcissistic personality disorder and pathological narcissism. In P. H. Blaney, R. F. Krueger, & T. Millon (Eds.), *Oxford textbook of psychopathology* (3rd ed.). Oxford University Press.

Ronningstam, E. (2005). *Identifying and understanding the narcissistic personality.* Oxford University Press.

Ronningstam, E. F. (2009). Narcissistic personality disorder: Facing DSM-V. *Psychiatric Annals, 39*(3), 111–121.

Rosenfeld, H. (1971). A clinical approach to the psychoanalytic theory of life and death instincts: An investigation into the aggressive aspects of narcissism. *International Journal of Psychoanalysis, 52*(2), 169–178.

Rosenfeld, H. (1987a). Afterthought: Changing theories and changing techniques. In *Impasse and interpretation: Therapeutic and anti-therapeutic factors in the psychoanalytic treatment of psychotic, borderline, and neurotic patients* (pp. 265–279). Tavistock.

Rosenfeld, H. (1987b). *Impasse and interpretation*. Tavistock.

Russ, E., Shedler, J., Bradley, R., & Westen, D. (2008). Refining the construct of narcissistic personality disorder: Diagnostic criteria and subtypes. *American Journal of Psychiatry*, *165*, 1473–1481.

Skodel, A. E., Morey, L. C., Bender, D. S., & Oldham, J. M. (2015). The alternative DSM-5 model for personality disorders: A clinical application. *American Journal of Psychiatry*, *172*(7), 606–613.

Smolewska, K., & Dion, K. L. (2005). Narcissism and adult attachment. *Self and Identity*, *4*, 59–68.

Wood, R. (2023). *A study of malignant narcissism: Personal and professional insights*. Routledge.

Zeigler-Hill, V., Green, B. A., Arnau, R. C., Sisemore, T. B., & Myers, E. M. (2011). Trouble ahead, trouble behind: Narcissism and early maladaptive schemas. *Journal of Behavior Therapy and Experimental Psychiatry*, *42*, 96–103.

Chapter 3

Clinical Examples of GN and VN

At this point, it feels appropriate to share clinical examples that the literature provides of grandiose narcissism (GN) and vulnerable narcissism (VN) so that the reader might better appreciate what these states look like in the real world of clinical encounters. The first two examples will be drawn from Bernardi and Eidlin's (2018) article in the International Journal of Psychoanalysis, "Thin-skinned or vulnerable narcissism and thick-skinned or grandiose narcissism: similarities and differences." The third, reflecting work with a patient diagnosed with malignant narcissism, comes from the Diamond et al. (2022) book, *Treating Pathological Narcissism with Transference-Focused Psychotherapy*.

The first case to be reviewed is of a woman, identified as "Mrs. A," whom Bernardi and Eidlin (2018) describe as being characterized by a predominantly GN position. In that sense, Mrs. A could be said to represent what many clinicians would regard as the prototypical or classical form of narcissism dominated by prominent investment in grandiosity. At the time that she chose to pursue treatment, she was 27 years old and was married with children.

I find Mrs. A especially instructive because she provides us with a portrait of what I think we expect to see clinically when the grandiosity that informs and defines a pathological self-structure faces significant compromise. Mrs. A presented in acute distress, struggling with significant depression and anxiety, painful somatic symptoms, severe emotional dysregulation (anger that pervaded all her relationships), pronounced sexual promiscuity, and a profound sense of shame and humiliation in association with a recent business failure. Around the time that her business failure unfolded, she also suffered an assault, her

DOI: 10.4324/9781032649535-3

father had endured a stroke, and her brother had been diagnosed with a dangerous form of cancer. Her personal presentation alternated between a haughty, contemptuous, arrogant posture in which she was dismissive of others and of her need for them versus a contrasting sense that she was terribly vulnerable and unsafe, surrounded by predatory figures who were likely to either exploit her and hurt her or discard her, perhaps in much the same way that she used her many lovers (she could brag that no one had ever left her; she had always left others, but first she would drive them wild with desire with her sexuality).

In the clinical description that was provided, which was very vividly drawn, one could almost feel Mrs. A's desperate attempts to re-establish grandiosity and dominance again; in the face of her expectation that she gave and gave and gave, only to find that others "took everything," she expressed a powerful desire to regain her dominion over others ("look, if they see you on the ground they step all over you, but if you're the powerful one, no one screws with you!!) (p. 299). The reversals that life had imposed upon her that began to shatter her grandiosity drew her into a painful, and humiliating, confrontation with her fears of being left alone. Notwithstanding the contempt that she relied upon to disqualify her husband's importance to her, there were moments when she felt all too keenly that she would miss his presence in her life. One got the sense that such a confrontation with her own dependent yearnings was searing for her, felt shameful, and almost catastrophically unbearable. Without the ascendancy she had managed to construct for herself before her world fell apart, it was as if she felt like a nobody, reflective, perhaps, of the kind of identity diffusion one would anticipate such a personality might experience should they lose the aggrandizement that created identity and cohesion for them. Her sense of self appeared to be entirely founded upon introjective strivings (confirmation of her self-reliance and self-directedness); in contrast, she seemed largely unable to make room for interdependence upon other people that would have been reflective of an ability to tolerate healthy anaclitic needs.

The sketch of her early years that was provided certainly helps one understand why she might have adopted such a position. When she was young, her father was said to have left the family for years while he was involved with a number of different women. Her depressed father could make her feel special ("the prettiest") when he was present in her life, but he could also subject her to "violent paternal interference that stripped her of everything." At times, she felt engulfed by rage which his abandonment had created for her. She was forced to help support the household economically and, perhaps like her mother, learned to detach herself from depth of emotional exchange, focusing upon practicalities that demanded her attention and assertion of her competence. One did not get a sense in reading this history that warmth, empathy, and expressions of deep caring were part of the family discourse. Mother did, apparently, convey appreciation for successes that the patient was able to realize, but there seems to have been an absence of meaningful celebration of Mrs. A's intrinsic value. Mrs. A seems to have played out her pain through poorly controlled acts of impulsivity and violence, use of drugs and alcohol, and marked instability in her relationships with her various boyfriends. Ambition, success, and entitlement eventually became defining for her, a safe place to consolidate identity and a sense that she was untouchable. She was indifferent to other's feelings and to the hurt that she might cause them by saying hurtful things to them; she became convinced of her own rightness and infallibility, insuring, in her terms, that the world could never take everything away from her again. It sounded as if she dealt with her own dependency needs by compulsively and derisively feeding those who came to her table to eat.

Having her world fall apart in the way that it did just prior to therapy must have felt like she was re-immersed in the experience that she had had as a helpless, defenseless child who couldn't count on the people around her to provide her with critical care in the form of stability and emotional sustenance that she, like any other child, understandably required. Tragically, it sounds like she never was able to trust the analytic process and invest in it in a way that would have permitted her to start to build constructive interdependencies in spite of the steadfastness of her analyst. Instead, she seems to have buffeted her therapist with much the same contempt and revulsion that she directed toward others, never really letting him/her in or him/her matter in a way that would have been healing for her. Once life circumstances allowed her to re-establish the ascendent posture that was so necessary for her to feel safe, she turned away from treatment. Her story inadvertently provides confirmation of why it is so hard for people bound together by grandiosity to allow themselves both to lean on others and to engage in deep exploration of the self. One can imagine that, were her grandiosity not compromised, she would likely never have sought out treatment for herself, in spite of the manifest damage she could see she was causing people around her. Such speculation is consistent with the literature (already reviewed) suggesting that people largely defined by VN orientation are much more likely to seek treatment for themselves than those largely defined by GN.

This clinical example also raises another interesting question in the literature: what does normal and pathological narcissism look like in women? Eva Lester (2000) attempts to address this issue in her eponymous article on the same subject. Following a fascinating discussion about fantasies of exceptionality that may form the basis for narcissistic yearning, she ties exceptionality to the wish for unification of opposing states (the wise baby, androgyny, reincarnation bridging life and death, etc.). The merging of opposites has been referred to as a desire for a mysterious unity. She references Bach (1977) quoting Eliade (1965, p. 291). Lester comments:

> It is here proposed that pregnancy and early infant care may represent a biologically determined and socially sanctioned partial gratification of the wish for mysterious unity that lies at the basis of many narcissistic fantasies... All point to the biological basis of the female's preparedness to enter into a specific form of relationship with the object. Such a relationship could be seen as the very prototype of the mysterious unity at the basis of all narcissistic wishes. It could be proposed that such preparedness and specificity of behaviors in the female may represent a measure of protection against the development of the grandiose self.... (p. 92)

Lester directs our attention to conclusions that Richman and Flaherty (1988) drew about their efforts to explore gender differences in a sample of first-year medical students:

> The sex differences involving the greater male prevalence of grandiosity, fantasies of unlimited success and lack of empathy, in contrast to the greater female experience of distress in response to the indifference of others, could be interpreted as consistent with the thesis that early object relations patterns give rise to exaggerated male needs for differentiation... and female needs for merger with objects. (pp. 375–376)

Lester felt that such findings echoed other research (Gilligan, 1982; LeVine, 1991; Stoller, 1976, 1985) that seemed to confirm "the female's greater need to maintain connection and communication within the existing object relations network in contrast to the male's need for separation from the primary object, exploration of the material world, and, often, tendency to establish dominance within the relational network" (p. 92). She also cited Notman and Nadelson's (1991) research that suggested an increased potential for greater connectedness to the caregiver in female infants than in males, who may experience early interaction with the mother as too arousing.

What's the import of such findings? Lester comments that "although narcissistic manifestations are not uncommon in women, the well articulated NPD is, it seems likely, a male personality disorder..." (p. 93). Her conclusion is consonant with Akhtar and Thompson's (1982) finding that female narcissism is "not in the literature... most of the patients who have been reported on are men" (p. 19). Both Mika (2017) and Wood (2023) have expressed the same opinion about more extreme forms of narcissism, malignant narcissism. So far as we can see, malignant narcissism appears to be an exclusively male experience. This "data," however, should be considered little better than anecdotal.

In this regard, I found it interesting that the dynamics which seemed to characterize Mrs. A's narcissistic personality disorder (NPD) incorporated strong albeit very ambivalently expressed anaclitic vulnerabilities, something which I typically don't observe in my male patients with NPD. Male vulnerability, including depression associated with NPD, assumes an angrier, more combative posture that tolerates little expressed need for other people. Again, this data is little better than anecdotal, but I think it is worth noting as a potential focus for future research and clinical observation.

As an interesting aside, the Lester article is also worth reading because it offers a fascinating portrait of Freud's Victorian attitudes toward women.

The next example that I would submit for consideration is one meant to capture the dynamics of VN. Like "Mrs. A," Mrs. B also comes from Bernardi and Eidlin (2018). These authors explained that they chose this case because it is one of the examples relied upon to establish the viability of VN as a diagnostic category in the *Diagnostic and Statistical Manual* (DSM). The case was originally cited in Skodel et al. (2015). Because the case material in Skodel is somewhat more detailed, I will rely on the case information provided in their article rather than exclusively on the case summary in Bernardi and Eidlin (2018).

Mrs. B, a 32-year-old white female, seems to have presented herself for treatment following a four-month bout of depression that was marked by feelings of emptiness, worthlessness, hypersomnia, poor concentration, diminished energy, modest weight gain, and ruminations about her childhood and early life. Depressive symptomatology also included thoughts of death and dying, but denial of suicidal ideation. Depression appears to have been precipitated by her failure to earn a promotion to partner in her law firm. Before depression manifested itself, it was preceded by anger, bitter disappointment, and shame.

The aforementioned depressive episode seems to have unfolded in a life context in which the patient felt herself to be generally dissatisfied, with the one exception of the academic proficiency she had demonstrated as a student and, more contemporaneously, her proficiency as an attorney. The patient stated that since her preteen years, she has felt personally unappealing to others and socially inept. Skodel et al. (2015) reported that "she does not understand how to relate to others or how others managed to make friends easily and to maintain long-lasting relationships" (p. 606). What sounded like powerful uneasiness about her own value meant that she avoided most social opportunities because she was afraid she would not be liked. She had never been in a relationship with a male partner, though she had been attracted to someone at one point, but she had been too frightened and ashamed to let this man know that she cared. She seems to have told herself, perhaps as compensation for the despair that she felt about the prospect of any future relationship, that she would be unlikely to find someone who met all of her demanding standards. It sounds like she tried to establish a sense of place or belonging with people in her surroundings by overextending herself and doing them favors, only to feel let down by the (for her) muted appreciation they directed toward her. Her handling of her interpersonal relations in her legal career sounded like an iteration of the same pattern: working in an assiduous, perfectionistic manner on any legal work that was assigned to her and then feeling let down by unappreciative others (colleagues) who experienced her as not getting through the relevant work quickly enough. The offset to the injury she seems to have endured was a sense that the caliber of her work was a cut above that of her colleagues; one also developed an impression from the patient summary that she may have been able to bolster self-esteem by carrying out invidious comparisons between her and her colleagues, reminding herself that her work was more ethically scrupulous than theirs.

Her growing-up experiences were characterized by her encounters with a mother who was struggling with chronic untreated depression that seems to have emerged around the time the first of her three sisters was born (the patient was the eldest). Mother could be scathingly critical, subject to angry outbursts, often referring to the patient as dumb or stupid in spite of her academic prowess. Mother's inability to appreciate her left her feeling deprived, depressed, and angry. Father was felt to be more accepting, but his availability and his support/protection seem to have been disrupted by his drinking. Perhaps attesting to the destructive impact of mother's moods and words and, possibly, the chaos that might have attended father's drinking, her childhood imbued her with a sense that the world was a dangerous place and that she was exceedingly vulnerable. It apparently became her role in the family to try to protect herself and others from the subjectively catastrophic shifts that occurred in the family by compulsively playing the role of family mediator. Her position as the eldest daughter in the family may have helped further consolidate her commitment to a mediator function. Doing so, possibly like the favors that she later did for friends and colleagues, was meant to win her reprieve and even approval from those people who were important to her. Notwithstanding the injury that her family caused her, the patient was said to prefer to spend most of her free time with them rather than trying to expand social options.

Bernardi and Eidlin (2018) argued that her personal challenges could best be understood not as social phobia or an avoidance disorder, but rather as a reflection of VN. They commented that "her sexual problem is related to her need to regulate her self-esteem through the approval of others. She needs her perfection to be confirmed – a difficult aspiration to perceive, as it remains covert and is only expressed through her self-imposed demands. She, thus, alternates between an expectation that her grandiose perfection will be acknowledged and a fear of experiences that will frustrate and shame her, hence she sees social withdrawal as a solution" (p. 301). They further suggested that because the patient could only see her own expectations rather than being able to recognize how other people saw/experienced her, she was not in a position to be able to mitigate her perceptions. Failure to see other people as they were rather than exclusively as a source of self-esteem affirmation ensured that she would face difficulty in establishing an intimate relationship. Put differently, I think they are suggesting that she carries on a relationship with her unrealistic expectations of others rather than with the real people around her.

My intention now is to offer an alternative perspective that I find more consonant with my own clinical experience. My comments are not intended to disqualify the thoughtful work that Bernardi and Eidlin (2018) and others like them have undertaken.

Having worked with people that I think come from similar backgrounds, what stands out for me is the potentially profound injury that people experience when they don't feel welcomed in their families and don't feel celebrated and embraced; the consequence is often a lasting difficulty in establishing a sense of belonging, place, and community in later life and in realizing a rewarding, sustaining sense of personal value informed by the affection and investment that important others make in us. As a result, such people feel shut out of the social world that other people seem to so easily inhabit. To use a simplistic metaphor, it's a little bit like standing outside a party watching other people enjoy one another without having any real sense of that which makes their social exchanges seemingly deeply rewarding. It's as if people feel permanently "othered," somehow excluded from experiencing the human connectedness that renders life so meaningful. They can simulate connection by contriving a presence that they imagine might work for them so that they can pass, but part of them recognizes that it's only a simulation and, at least unconsciously, expect to be found out. Extending the role of mediator and of academic excellence that she was able to realize earlier in her life offers a kind of compensation for "B," but certainly not a "good enough" one; one can imagine that she struggles with an underlying sense both that she will never be entirely acceptable to others and that the rage, disdain, and sadness that her impossible position creates for her must be all too close to the surface, further exacerbating her fears about belonging. From one perspective, she can be seen to be trying to heal a profound narcissistic injury in the only way that feels safe to her, by over-functioning.

While there are elements of what could be referred to as grandiosity in her character structure, I think it plays a very peripheral role. What I think I see is a deeply traumatized person who is living with very imposing pain indeed. I can't find justification for identifying her as narcissistic. Her "narcissism" consists of trying to hang onto the only qualities that have served to establish the limited means of human connection of which she is capable. To be sure, she has endured a significant narcissistic injury and she is isolated and cut off both from others and from her own feeling life, but that would also not be sufficient to convince me it would be helpful for me to think of her as narcissistic.

Just because narcissistic injury has played a pivotal role in one's pain does not mean that one is fated to become narcissistic oneself.

As an aside, I see the nature of injury B is experiencing as frequently arising in the context of both early loss and/or significantly depressed moms who, by virtue of their depression, may tragically not be able to make an adequate investment in their children.

As I am writing this passage, I also have to acknowledge to myself and to my reader that I think of narcissistic disorders as being fundamentally and decisively oriented around investment in a grandiose self. The thought also occurs to me that the nature of "B's" pain and the narcissistic injury she has sustained has led me into what would, in many respects, essentially be considered a Kohutian formulation of this woman's life experience. On reflection, it strikes me that Kohutian formulations allow me to best appreciate dynamics that are seen to drive what is being called VN; a Kernbergian perspective, on the other hand, appears to do the best job capturing dynamic forces that predominate in what we've referenced as GN. I will say more about these ideas in Chapter 4 as I review Daniel Shaw's and my own conceptions of narcissism. For the moment, however, let's now look at a clinical example of malignant narcissism that Diamond et al. (2022) provide in their new book.

I have chosen Diamond et al.'s (2022) book as a source for an example of malignant narcissism for two reasons: first, perhaps because malignant narcissists are unlikely to enter treatment, there are few rich, detailed clinical examples of extended treatment engagement to be found and second, because the example that Diamond et al. (2022) provide is considered within a Kernbergian formulation, it allows us to remain within the boundaries of Kernberg's theoretical work, which is, broadly speaking, where I'd like to focus our attention before moving on to my own work and Daniel Shaw's.

"Michael" is the case study which the Diamond et al. group cites as an example of malignant narcissism. He is described as struggling with malignant narcissism within the context of overall functioning at a borderline level. The formal descriptor they employed is malignant narcissism with Borderline Personality Organization. This mode of categorization is somewhat confusing. In their original schema, they denoted three levels of functioning that could be seen to characterize narcissistic adjustment: higher level function, borderline level function, and malignant narcissism wherein each level represents a deterioration in "quality of object relations, capacity for intimacy and moral functioning, and increasing aggression and envy" (p. 53). Their framing of their diagnosis suggests that borderline level functioning, at least, and malignant narcissism are entities that can be conceived as being orthogonal to one another.

Michael is said to be a gifted young man in his 20s who maintained grandiose expectations for a nascent art career that he had been unable to realize for himself. He seemed to repeatedly sabotage the promising opportunities that his talent created for himself. His personal history was marked by multiple self-injurious behaviors that had unfolded over an extended course of time, an inclination to engage in exploitative relationships with others, substance abuse, bouts of depression and anxiety, and several hospitalizations for suicidality. What sounded like extensive outpatient intervention had failed to stabilize him and/or ameliorate the intensity of his symptom picture. Self-injurious behavior included lacerating his arms and legs. He fell in love at 23, marrying a woman from a socially prominent family who supported him financially and who attributed his erratic behavior to an artistic temperament. During the course of this relationship, he was described as being chronically unfaithful. He refused to indulge his wife's wish to have a child because he believed he was "too sick" to become a father. It was in this context that he was referred for transference-focused psychotherapy which the Weill Cornell group subsequently provided.

His mother had suffered a catastrophic car accident when Michael was five, resulting in the loss of Michael's younger brother and in his mother becoming clinically depressed. As a result, she became unable to look after Michael, instead relying upon him for both emotional support and caregiving. She was also characterized as "inappropriately seductive, at times exposing herself to Michael and demanding that he put her to bed" (p. 15). His caregiving burdens were compounded by a father who, as a successful executive, was fated to often travel away from home to meet his business obligations. When present, father could affirm Michael's formidable talents as an artist, performer, and athlete, underscoring that his unique abilities destined him for special achievement. Father was also given to drink heavily and to find himself consumed with rage that could consummate in physical abuse directed toward Michael. On one such occasion, father had murdered the patient's pet birds.

The case material included careful documentation of various salient aspects of Michael's treatment relationship and his eventual progress in therapy. Therapy had unfolded over the course of some four years before terminating via mutual consent. The early years of treatment were apparently quite stormy, very quickly dominated by severe acting out, some of which potentially constituted meaningful threat for the therapist and/or for the patient. As an example, the patient told the therapist that he and the woman that he was having an affair with planned a double murder-suicide pact to be carried out in the therapist's office. The story was apparently related with a sense of glee and excitement. The idea that the patient and his girlfriend could pull off the murder-suicide successfully even after having told the therapist of his plan seemed particularly pleasing to him. Michael evidently anticipated that enacting his plan would leave the therapist feeling both fearful and humiliated. On another occasion, Michael told the therapist that he had a box cutter on his person and hadn't yet decided if he should hurt her during their meeting. It was felt that these incidents were reflection of a "sense of grandiosity... infused with ego syntonic aggression fueled by paranoid feelings that the therapist might harm and injure him – beliefs that he used to justify his callous manipulation of the therapist and others, and his potentially harmful actions – all of which characterize the syndrome of malignant narcissism" (p. 16).

As therapy progressed, it sounded as if Michael's fear of being harmed by a tyrannical therapist on whom he projected his destructive impulses became more transparent. Michael's threatening behaviors could be seen as an attempt to neutralize a threatening other through control, debasement, and threat. The Diamond et al. group believed that these dynamics were fueled by representations of the persecutor/victim dyad that had defined so much of his interaction with his parents. At times Michael played out the role of persecutor himself, though probably not with full or even partial awareness of the fear that was driving him; at other times, he experienced himself as vulnerable and as targeted, though so far as I could see, that was less true of his presentation during the earlier part of treatment work. As therapy progressed, the therapist was able to focus on "the destructive aspects of his identification with powerful, punitive internal objects – the seductive, but neglectful maternal figure and the abusive paternal figure. The therapist further explored how the power of these internal representations... kept (Michael) from forming a genuine emotional connection with the therapist..." (p. 381). Michael was so compelled by his fear that he would be violated again as he had been when he was younger that he couldn't afford to surrender his grandiosity and his threatening posture. It simply didn't feel safe enough, in other words, for him to do so. It was only as the therapist could respond with equanimity to Michael's threats and was, simultaneously, able to set boundaries (a point of emphasis for the Diamond et al. group) that Michael could both better articulate the nature of his fear and tolerate greater interdependence and vulnerability with the therapist. Doing so eventually unearthed Michael's own fears that he had internalized parental cruelty and harmed others in his attempts to protect himself in much the same way that his parents had harmed him. Regret and remorse thereby established themselves as a greater presence in the therapeutic alliance. The Diamond et al. group underscored that it is only in the end stages of treatment that patients become aware of the genetic linkages that compel them to act as they do. As Michael was able to feel his way through some of these linkages (ties between past and present), consolidating his grasp of them, he became able to invest in his marriage in a meaningful way and to take on a role as a father.

To my mind, Michael's progression toward genuine interrelatedness and gratifying interdependence is a very plausible account of a powerful therapeutic process that unfolded with his therapist. To maintain the measure of equanimity and self-possession that Michael's therapist was able to realize in the context of an oftentimes threatening and chaotic transference/countertransference relationship is quite an inspiring and courageous undertaking and certainly a testament to the therapist's own humanity. As Kernberg himself has so often commented, being targeted by threat and by toxic ascriptions in a volatile, labile relationship with a patient dissuades many a therapist from continuing on with their work. Having to contend with an array of sadistic, retaliatory feelings/fantasies that alternate with the wish to rescue side-by-side the sense that one is guilty of being either (or both) a bad or an inadequate therapist offers further inducements to break away from what feels like an unbearable treatment process. Add to this the re-traumatization that is inevitably a part of the countertransference response – reflecting incitement of vulnerabilities that the therapist carries within him or her reflective of their own trauma experiences – and one has a sense of just how demanding work with this class of patients really is. One knows that if one does back off, unless one is part of an exceptional group of clinicians who do a lot of this kind of work, it will be almost impossible to find someone else willing to step in and assume the burdens that working with this group of patients entails.

I wonder if Michael was able to make such wonderful progress in his therapy because, although he could be described as malignantly narcissistic, vulnerability was an obviously pronounced part of his clinical profile. As such, the "healthy" part of him that could seek out and eventually accept sustenance from another was more accessible; in my experience, patients who have rigidly organized themselves around their grandiosity and their intolerance of dependence either do not solicit treatment for themselves or, alternatively, if they find themselves in treatment (often because they have been compelled to come by others), they find it extraordinarily difficult to move past their paranoia and their mistrust; the brutish projective identification that they attempt to invest the therapist with overwhelms them if not their perspective therapeutic collaborator, rendering a meaningful therapeutic alliance utterly out of reach. I'm sure it must feel like the therapist both evokes unbearable envy (because the therapist is capable of feeling and being alive while the malignant narcissist, in the main, is not) at the same time that the patient experiences the therapist as trying to rob him of the few "assets" he possesses.

Interestingly, the Diamond et al. group's description of Michael's therapeutic progression included idealization of the therapist and internalization of the therapist's composure and analytic attitude, perhaps contributing to the formation of a more realistic idealized self. In this sense, one could hear elements, at least, of Kohutian conceptions of therapeutic growth. In the main, however, the Kernbergian or object relations approach to conceptualization and treatment of malignant narcissism seemed to be more helpful than a Kohutian paradigm.

References

Akhtar, S., & Thomson, J. J. (1982). Overview: Narcissistic personality disorder. *American Journal of Psychiatry*, *139*(1), 12–20.

Bach, S. (1977). On narcissistic fantasies. *International Review of Psychoanalysis*, *4*, 281–293.

Bernardi, R., & Eidlin, M. (2018). Thin-skinned or vulnerable narcissism and thick-skinned or grandiose narcissism: Similarities and differences. *International Journal of Psychoanalysis*, *99*(2), 291–313.

Diamond, D., Yeomans, F. E., Stern, B. L., & Kernberg O. F. (2022). *Treating pathological narcissism with transference-focused psychotherapy*. The Guilford Press.

Eliade, M. (1965). *The two and the one*. Harper Torchbooks.

Gilligan, C. (1982). *In a different voice: Psychological theory and Women's development*. Harvard University Press.

Lester, L. (2000). Normal and pathological narcissism in women. Changing Ideas in a Changing World: The Revolution in Psychoanalysis: Essays in Honour of Arnold Cooper (87—93). Karnac Books.

LeVine, R. A. (1991). Gender differences. Interpreting anthropological data. In M. T. Notman & C. Nadelson (Eds.), *Women and men*. American Psychiatric Press.

Mika, E. (2017). Who goes Trump? Tyranny as a triumph of narcissism. In B. Lee (Ed.), *The dangerous case of Donald Trump* (2nd ed., pp. 289–308). Thomas Dunne Books.

Notman, M. T., & Nadelson, C. (1991). *A review of gender behavior in women and men*. American Psychiatric Press.

Richman, J. A., & Flaherty, J. A. (1988). "Tragic man" and "tragic woman": Gender differences in narcissistic styles. *Psychiatry, 51*, 368–377.

Skodel, A. E., Morey, L. C., Bender, D. S., & Oldham, J. M. (2015). The alternative DSM-5 model for personality disorders: A clinical application. *American Journal of Psychiatry, 172*(7), 606–613.

Stoller, R. J. (1976). Primary femininity. *Journal of the American Psychoanalytic Association, 24*(5 Suppl), 59–78.

Stoller, R. J. (1985). *Observing the erotic imagination*. Yale University Press.

Wood, R. (2023). *A study of malignant narcissism: Personal and professional insights*. Routledge.

Chapter 4

Alternative Conceptions of the VN/GN Relationship

Now, I have the pleasure of reintroducing the reader to some of the confusion and ambiguity that has typified our understanding of narcissism. I will turn to the work of Daniel Shaw and to my own work to offer an alternative conceptualization of VN. Doing so will draw us into a reconsideration of GN as well. Please keep in mind that seemingly opposing formulations are not meant to displace one another, but, rather, can serve to provide us with differing perspectives whose clinical utility may vary depending upon the challenges that a given patient presents us.

In his 2014 book, *Traumatic Narcissism,* psychoanalyst Daniel Shaw employed the term traumatizing narcissism so that it might be distinguished from other forms of narcissism that denoted vulnerability, such as Bach's deflated narcissist, Kohut's shame-prone narcissist, and Rosenfeld thin-skinned narcissist. He wrote:

> The term "pathological narcissist," often used to describe this set of character structures, is also used, problematically, to label and describe the people he typically exploits and victimizes, whose sense of self-esteem he has dramatically destabilized.

> (Shaw, 2014, p. 11)

Later in his book, he elaborated:

> I have never been comfortable with calling all these kinds of people pathological. The patient who is labeled the deflated, thin-skinned pathological narcissist is usually someone who in development has suffered severe damage to their self-esteem system, and whose self-esteem

DOI: 10.4324/9781032649535-4

regulation is therefore inconsistent and precarious, subject to the internal persecution of the split off protector self. In my view, this person is more aptly deemed a sufferer of cumulative, developmental, posttraumatic stress. These patients are inhabited and often tormented by the ghosts of their traumatizers. To struggle desperately to regulate one's self-esteem, become lost and hopeless about being loved and desired, to fear that only by subjugating oneself to seemingly more powerful others can one hope to be able to rely on human connection – these are survival attempts for people whose sense of subjectivity has been dramatically co-opted, who cannot confer legitimacy upon themselves, but must go begging for it from others. Speaking of these developmentally traumatized patients as pathological is sharply discordant to the ways that most psychoanalysts speak of any other traumatized patients. (p. 10)

It may make sense to divert some attention to Shaw's use of the term "protector/prosecutor self," which was developed by Howell (2005) and Kalsched (1996). This powerful term refers to the internalization of the traumatizing narcissist's envious voice that creates a powerful, prosecutorial presence inside a targeted individual. Now any time the self becomes too big, too ambitious, too well articulated, too independent, the internalized representation of the prosecutorial other attacks, diminishing, humiliating, and undermining hope at precisely the point that growth begins to proffer itself. It is as if an affected individual re-imagines and re-enlivens the persecutory narcissistic voice as a means of warning him or herself that they are wandering into territory that would offend the narcissistic presence in their life. Self-diminishment becomes self-protective. As Shaw notes, the internalized persecutorial voice is an extension of the sufferer's internalized version of the person or persons constituting their narcissistic surround; as such, it may be a harsher and more intractable version of the caustic other that they carry inside them and, I would say, as an aside, may be infected with their own poorly recognized rage deriving from the many injuries their personhood has endured. Accordingly, the persecutorial voice can be quite raw and searing, as the examples which Shaw provides attest to: "You nothing, you loser! No one could or would ever love you, you're disgusting! Give up!" (p. 8). Parenthetically, I would agree with Shaw, but would add that the persecutorial voice can manifest itself more imposingly in intricate, condemnatory, threatening fantasies people can find challenging to separate themselves from.

Shaw believed (as I do) that the need to love and be loved and the need to have one's subjectivity recognized and affirmed were seminal human needs that play a crucial role in the construction of the self. Failure to have these needs met distorted the self through repetitive relational trauma. Of course, the reader will note that, in many ways, this formulation is similar to Kohut's conception of critical empathic failures that inflict repetitive injuries throughout the course of the child's relational experience, producing errant and often self- and other- destructive attempts to repair injury to the child's early aspirational, grandiose strivings. Consider now Shaw's description of a healthy developmental process:

"Children also naturally seek to be admired and applauded as they spread their wings and express their exhibitionistic, grandiose tendencies (as especially emphasized by Kohut). I think of developmental grandiosity as self-idealization, something most children do naturally, if allowed, as they dance all around the house like ballerinas, sing like American idols, stare at the mirror waiting to see if they have washboard abs yet, and so on. They are naturally developing, if allowed to, 'their love affair with the world,' as stormy as that affair can become, especially during adolescence" (pp. 13–14). Shaw pointed out that the idea "children naturally, not pathologically, seek to feel accepted by and made part of the idealized parent's world" (p. 13) was one that had been widely discussed by numbers of psychoanalytic theorists including Ferenczi, Suttie, Fairbairn, Winnicot, Balint, Bowlby, and Kohut, as a partial list that Shaw provided.

That such grandiosity could be expected to re-emerge in treatment was given for Shaw. Though he did not say so explicitly, one understood that for him, it represented the frustrated strivings of an unrequited life, much, in some ways, like Kohut's tragic man. Such strivings could be expected to become more pronounced as patients felt safe enough in treatment to dare to experience hope about themselves – hope that promised to free them from the spiritual imprisonment and violation that they had endured and hope that could be expected to inspire fear, self-diminishment, and self-initiated persecutorial attack. Patients who dared to hope that they could aspire to be more than they were might also find themselves subject to poorly recognized dread that the therapist might engage in retaliatory counterattack, much like the narcissistic other. For some patients, "the (grandiose) fantasy could feel dangerously out of control, and it always ended with deflation" (p. 112). Later, Shaw added: "these grandiose fantasy moments I have experienced with patients have often marked a turning point in the treatment – a way towards an ending. The fantasy stops being shameful; some of the potentials that were abandoned because they seem ridiculously grandiose can be salvaged and put to constructive, creative use" (p. 113). Shaw did caution that "as these patients end therapy, they usually feel some wariness, trying to hold onto faith in themselves, hoping they can keep growing without slipping backward too much, for too long. They expect ups and downs, but better handled ones" (p. 113). Even under adventitious circumstances, then, the persecutorial voice can persist, though perhaps with less effect.

The other kind of injury that Shaw emphasizes that people endure as part of narcissistic predation is what Shaw describes as a rape of personhood, or, using Shengold's (1989) term, "soul murder." Shengold defined soul murder as "the deliberate attempt to eradicate or compromise the separate identity of another person" (p. 2). While Shaw took issue with the characterization of such psychological violence as deliberate, seeing the actions of the traumatizing narcissist as informed instead by "a delusional conviction of righteousness" (p. 149), he did recognize soul murder, like denial of recognition, as a nearly unbearable act that created terrible compromise for the person who had to live with its consequences. Implicit in his discussion about soul murder was the assumption that such an injury was actually a series of injuries that had played themselves out in the individual's larger relational context. For me, the concept of soul murder gives greater shape and meaning to Kohut's phrase, empathic failure. As Shaw alluded to at several points in his book, without saying so explicitly, it gives rise to a disturbingly depleted, tenuous, resentful feeling of self that infiltrates and defines people's ongoing subjectivity.

In summarizing the relational system that the traumatizing narcissist builds, Shaw considered four factors to be important: (1) the traumatizing narcissist was likely a victim of relational trauma of one kind or another themselves; (2) the traumatizing narcissist is possessed of a delusional sense of infallibility and entitlement; (3) dependency needs and the shame that they produced were to be externalized onto others; and (4) the traumatizing narcissist was committed to suppression of the others' subjectivity.

In considering receptivity to treatment, Shaw observed that "the overinflated, traumatizing narcissist is far less likely to present for treatment than the person that he has traumatized; and that the traumatized person is often viewed as a narcissistic patient, when it would be clinically more accurate to recognize her as a trauma survivor" (p. 17). Like Rosenfeld, Shaw added that such trauma survivors "can prove to be quite challenging to work with, can be quite masochistic, self-and-other destructive, and intractably depressed" (p. 17). The therapeutic task with such a deflated patient was to "help her discover and define her own subjectivity, and to become freer from undue concern with a fear of the other's needs, expectations, and judgements" (p. 17).

The therapeutic goal, in other words, was to enable her to experience herself as a subject in her own life in a way that it would be possible "to have a consistent enough sense of one's intrinsic worth and value, to know what one thinks and feels, what one wants and doesn't want; to feel permitted, or free, to assert the legitimacy of one's own point of view, without having either to deny the reality of others or to adopt the other's reality for fear of being isolated, or at worst, annihilated" (pp. 18–19). As a subject, one could be free to experience desire oneself "as an agent capable of meaningful and productive action" (p. 19). Part of the therapist's task was to ensure that therapist and patient were not caught in cycles of "complementarity" in which the therapeutic relationship was defined by alternating cycles of domination and subjugation; on the contrary, through careful attendance to his own countertransference and the needs of the patient, it was hoped that therapy could be defined by mutuality in which both parties had room to experience their own uniqueness and express it. Parenthetically, Shaw's comments about complementarity reminded one of Bach's conception of narcissistic transference as moving back and forth between polarized impulses of dominance and submission. Bach, however, made his comments in the context of reference to movement between a defensively hyper-cathected sadistic grandiose self and a defensively hyper-cathected idealized object to which he masochistically submits – a vacillation, I would think, that would most likely present itself in the context of decisive GN (where a sadistic grandiose self is most likely to present itself) rather than VN (Bach & Schwartz, 1972).

In Shaw's framework, inevitable empathic failures could be addressed and repaired, further confirming for the patient who had suffered narcissistic violation that identity and voice were precious and could be respected and celebrated. In Shaw's terms, the kind of analytic processes described construed analysis as an act of love that had the potential to heal damaged subjectivity that the traumatizing narcissist had inflicted on people close to him. It meant that an important part of the analyst's task was to help his patient free the self "from the shame of feeling at fault for being unloved and (from) a life of post-traumatic self-negation" (p. 34)

Shaw has offered us an important alternative way to organize our ideas about vulnerable narcissism and our appreciation of its phenomenology. Like Shaw, I very much agree that it is misleading to think of such people as being narcissistic, as will become apparent as I talk about my own conceptions of individuals who have faced repeated relational violations by a narcissist. Before doing so, I would like to dwell for a moment on Shaw's understanding of what a traumatizing narcissist is.

Shaw hoped that the term traumatic narcissism freed his conception of narcissism from the pejorative implications of terms like "pathological" and "malignant." He strongly believed that traumatizing narcissists who injured others were deserving of the right to be understood in much the same way that any of the other people we work with are. He anticipated that in-depth understanding would enable us to regard such people with compassion, seeing them as profoundly injured human beings whose damaging relational experiences had likely played a crucial role in establishing their destructiveness.

Shaw tells us the term traumatizing narcissism was a replacement for two terms he previously used to describe the same phenomenon: pathological narcissism and malignant narcissism. It is not entirely clear that the clinical entity Shaw is referring to is meant to capture an extreme form of narcissism, as malignant narcissism typically does, or whether, more generically, he means to draw us into a discussion about pathological narcissism, which may be more similar in form to narcissistic personality disorder (NPD), a less forbidding diagnosis. His appreciation of traumatizing narcissism derives, at least in part, from his experiences in dealing with a cult leader who dramatically impacted his own life. As one reads about this leader's personality, one is left with the impression that the concept Shaw has pieced together is closer in nature to more extreme forms of narcissism. It would appear to differ from a Kernbergian conception of malignant narcissism, at least in limited respects. To remind the reader, Kernberg would say that pathological narcissism is defined by the core features of this disorder (prominent exploitativeness, self-centeredness, entitlement, and interpersonal antagonism) in the company of "(1) intense paranoid characterological features, (2) ego syntonic aggression against others and/or self with an emphasis on defeating others, and (3) antisocial behavior"

(Diamond et al. 2022, p. 357). Like Kernberg, Shaw's grasp of traumatizing narcissism certainly acknowledges the presence of strong paranoid elements as well as unconscious sadistic elements, but he would not see sadism as deliberately enacted by people he regards as traumatizing narcissists, viewing them instead, as previously noted, as compelled by a delusional conviction of their own righteousness.

Shaw provides us with his definition of the type of narcissism he is trying to capture with the term traumatizing narcissism:

> I am especially focusing on a particular type of the predominantly overinflated, entitled, grandiose narcissist, in the way in which this person characteristically organizes relationships. I call this person the "traumatic narcissist." In what I (Shaw, 2010) have previously termed "the pathological narcissist's relational system," I described the narcissist who seeks hegemony for his subjectivity by weakening and suppressing the subjectivity of the other for the purpose of control and exploitation. The other is then left in grave doubt about the validity and even the reality of their own subjectivity. This sadistic, abusive aspect of narcissism stems from the belief, often held unconsciously, that the separate subjectivity of the other is a threat to the survival, literally and/or figuratively, of one's own subjectivity – and the other must therefore be captured and kept under control. (p. 12)

In the form of narcissism that Shaw is drawing our attention to, the destruction of voice and subjectivity describes the core nature of injury that the traumatizing narcissist inflicts on those around him. The implication is that being targeted for predation by a traumatizing narcissist is likely to create profound jeopardy for one's sense of self. Shaw emphasizes that the nature of such injury is traumatic and that it produces a chronically vulnerable individual who doesn't feel safe in the world, who is afraid of being re-traumatized, and who likely feels that they lack the means to navigate their way through life with the meager resources that the traumatizing narcissist has left them.

Compare, now, Shaw's formulation of traumatizing narcissism with my own of malignant narcissism. My formulation derives from the experience of having grown up with a malignantly narcissistic father and having had the opportunity to work, over the course of 50 years of practice, with six patients I regarded as malignantly narcissistic. Like many other practitioners, I also worked with patients that could be described as possessing NPD and/or people who had been wounded or traumatized by narcissistic family members. Typically, people with NPD did not stay long in treatment, expending effort to undermine my relationship with the family member that I was working with or, alternatively, participating in treatment only briefly before backing away from it. In my book, *A Study of Malignant Narcissism: Personal and Professional Insights* (Routledge 2023), I outline my conceptions of malignant narcissism at some length. I begin with my appreciation of the origins of malignant narcissism, moving on subsequently to a description of what I have come to understand malignant narcissism is:

> … One powerful dynamic seemed to stand out in great relief: relentless, ruthless early exploitation and adultification of a target individual by parental figures…parents were experienced as making unceasing, punishing demands that their needs and their agendas be attended to while providing little sustenance for their child and little recognition of the child's own needs. The level of expectation and commitment that parents imposed upon their children gave little quarter, allowing a child no room to be a child and become the child that they might have been. All was duty. All was work. All was obligation. Listening to these histories was hard. Children dedicated and rededicated themselves to their parents' purpose without receiving much reward, save either indirect or lavishly indulgent confirmation that their soul destroying effort made them special. Either directly or indirectly (but more typically the former) aggrandizement and grandiosity were the close companions of exhaustion…
>
> As a result of such an experience, love comes to connote toxicity, signifying obligation, exploitation, and terrifying levels of psychic depletion that increasingly confirm love as a dangerous and jeopardizing experience for the self. Others' demands create a measure of psychic and … physical starvation that is felt to threaten annihilation, if not of the person, then of the spirit. Such starvation occurs in the context in which the parental other is felt to be relatively indifferent or at least insensitive to the child's literal struggle for survival… As exploitation continues, extending itself throughout childhood and even young adulthood, deep and intractable cynicism about the possibility of generosity and meaningful,

sustaining caring from others entrenches itself. It is, increasingly, supported by vigilance meant to ensure that the self never lets down its guard, that it never lets others gain traction through love, and that invocation of mistrust is immediate, pervasive, and unyielding. The self has to ensure that it cannot be touched by human hand or heart. The self that emerges is formidably alone and formidably self-interested, determined never again to expose itself to the exploitation and depredation of others.

(Wood, 2023, p. 148)

I elaborated further:

The emergent self is also profoundly mistrustful of dependence on others, having rarely experienced dependence as a constructive and fulfilling enterprise. The inaccessibility of interdependence ensures that solitude becomes more formidable. The terrified, lonely child seizes upon the self-aggrandizement and grandiosity assigned it, clinging to it as a bulwark against all the unrequited need piling up inside that the child has had little opportunity to gratify. Aggrandizement also seems to offer protection against the suffocating helplessness that the child's devastating circumstances have created. "If I can pretend that I'm bigger, that I am more than the defenseless child that I am, if I can believe in my aggrandizement, I can feel safer." Aggrandizement and grandiosity further offer promise that the child can somehow satisfy its needy parent, consolidating connection and belonging and, perhaps, ensuring parental survival. Most importantly – and perhaps more poignantly – the aggrandized self is relied upon to protect the child from too close an acquaintance with the damaged, neglected inadequate self that exists under the surface – the frightened child who is beset by unbearable vulnerabilities.

(Wood, 2023, p. 148)

I would further suggest that such a child may feel poorly articulated shame that they have not been truly loved, shame which intertwines with the sense that they are profoundly disposable and, at the same time, profoundly special and indispensable. As such a child begin to separate themselves from human connection, their starvation and its progeny, rapacity and envy, only intensify, producing a person who attempts to fill themselves with vestiges of money, power, status, and fame in an effort to address the growing void inside that sustaining relationships with others might have otherwise addressed. The emergent self has little tolerance for others' voices and needs, compelled, as an act of self-preservation and an attempt to protect itself from further trauma, to dominate, subjugate, and exploit those around it to confirm that it is safe from reciprocal attack. A well of rage that is never far from the surface becomes a prominent and defining part of the self, a protective wall that keeps others out. As the acts of devastation and predation it must commit pile up inside (see our discussion of Kernberg), the self's internal world and the world around it begin to coalesce, eventuating in a deeply paranoid posture that traps the self in a projected world. Now, the self seemingly has confirmation that others are as predatory as it is, confirmation that sustains formidable entitlement. In consequence, the self becomes hypervigilant, ready to attack and disable the other or to exploit them; all is action and combat. Nuanced thought, discernment, weighted judgment, and empathy represent impediments that potentially disable the self. Relationships are compulsively tested. Those who do not accommodate the malignant narcissist's interpretations of reality, distorted as they are by malevolent self-interest, are quickly discarded or annihilated, as is any voice that shows opposition to the narcissist's perspectives and prerogatives. Rationality and science offend, as do voices that appeal to decency and civility.

Just as fear infiltrates and defines the war footing that the malignant narcissist requires of himself to feel prepared to contend with encroachment from a rapacious world, so, too, does it infuse the lives of the people who share space with him. Safety is to be found by twinning oneself with the narcissist's bigotries and hatreds and by aligning oneself with his grandiosity. Denied decency, generosity, and love, the malignantly narcissistic personality seeks to deconstruct those qualities in others, reconfiguring the wasteland that exists in his interior in theirs.

Defenses like projective identification and splitting help him achieve these ends as he assigns others the ugly intentionalities and feeling states that define him. Projective identification is characterized as a process in which an individual not only ascribes his own malign intent to someone else, but then induces them to act it out – confirming his original impressions of them. The best example of projective identification that I can offer is embedded in a Dennis the Menace cartoon in which Dennis tells his father, "it all started when he hit me back" (Dr. Paul Van Wyke, private communication). In my terms, projective identification is not only an unconscious process (the classical view) but, rather, one in which the narcissist may quite deliberately infect others with the darkness that engulfs him, particularly if in doing so, he is serving some transactional end. In such a fashion, others he sees as standing in his way can be identified as contemptible and as enemies to be destroyed or depreciated. So far as I can see, the line between conscious and unconscious process becomes quite blurry indeed as one considers the depredations that the malignant narcissist enacts. In a world held together by the fear that he generates, the malignant narcissist needs enemies for others to attack; through the use of defenses like projective identification and splitting, he can readily create them.

Berke (1985) has powerfully captured the linkage between projective identification and envy, a core affect that defines malignant narcissism:

> Simultaneously and eventually (the envier) seeks totally to alter and rubbish the object, to destroy any goodness in it and control it so it can't fight back. To accomplish this the envier uses an offensive maneuver by which a person manipulates words, thoughts, actions or moods to put himself, or a part of himself, into another (person, thing, mental representation) and to combine with it. Projective identification is both a perceptual transformation and an interpersonal transaction. From the standpoint of the subject (the envier), the envied then no longer exists in its own right. The envier "sees" and believes that the person or thing is identical with what he has put into it or attributed to it... The envied person may have an inexplicable sense of being or feeling different... If the behavior strikes a certain cord, then slowly, involuntarily, the envied "victim" will begin to feel, think and act as the envier sees him ... The experience is like being under attack from powerful, hostile forces which intend to drive one mad and destroy one's mind, a view not far from the truth. (pp. 176–177)

In another passage, Berke states, simply, that "envious tension is aroused by awareness of vitality and prosperity, indeed by life itself" (p. 174). Equally poignantly, Ian Hughes (private conversation, 2022) summarized his grasp of what he understood envy to be after reading my book, *A Study of Malignant Narcissism:* "evil can be construed as envy of love."

I would like to comment now on the vacillation between GN and VN states that one sees in malignant narcissism. I very much agree that such vacillations occur, though I would perhaps characterize them differently than some of the other clinicians whose work I have reviewed. As I have already made clear, I see pathological narcissists and more extreme forms of narcissism like malignant narcissism, as being consolidated around a grandiose self that dominates identity. At the same time, I recognize that people who are largely defined by their grandiosity also demonstrate acute displays of vulnerability whenever they face challenges from other people. Such vulnerability is typically expressed as retaliatory rage towards an offending party. Occasionally, rage associated with such vulnerability may be infected with childish petulance that may have the effect of rendering such rage absurd and hyperbolized, but for the most part it comprises a rageful storm that is meant to shock and awe and that certainly contains lethality of intention. Sometimes such rageful displays are essentially transactional, calculated to disorganize and immobilize the other party. Real vulnerability largely eludes personalities built around grandiosity; that is, only rarely does the grandiose narcissist re-experience the helplessness and hopelessness that characterized his originally traumatic childhood relational traumas. When his vulnerability assumes that aspect, the grandiose narcissist is truly at risk, subjectively experiencing catastrophic disintegration of the self and, often, associated suicidal risk, which can result in both self and other destructive behavior.

There is a great deal in my formulation that I have not described, and that space will not permit. As I have with other theorists, I have attempted to touch those facets of my conceptualization that are most salient. There is only one other dimension of malignant narcissism that I think it is important to mention – contrivance. Because the malignant narcissist is not privy to the gentle and sustaining music that defines human interaction characterized by love, generosity, acknowledgment of vulnerability, the capacity to laugh at oneself, to acknowledge missteps and foibles, etc., he has to feign his humanity, approximating what he thinks the human response ought to be rather than feeling it. Bach (1975) has written an important paper called "Narcissism, Continuity and the Uncanny". In his paper, he attempts to capture what might be meant by the "uncanny," calling attention to the uncanny experience we encounter in ourselves as we watch a man who is able to imitate a machine. Later in his article, he asks us to consider that what is missing in the interaction between a surrogate mother and a rhesus monkey baby is lack of reciprocity and, perhaps even more importantly, "a dialogue of action and response, which goes on in the form of a circular process within the dyad, as a continuous, mutually stimulating feedback circuit…" (cited by Bach in Spitz, 1963, pp. 162–166). Spitz adds that it is only between two living partners that such processes can take place and that they are, therefore, suitable to serve to distinguish the living from the inanimate. Perhaps a subtle point, but one that strikes me as profoundly important.

From my perspective, pathological narcissism and its more severe cousin, malignant narcissism, both isolate the sufferer from the world of human connection, forcing them to simulate and contrive relationships rather than being moved by the sustaining emotional interchanges that flow back and forth between people who have the capacity to genuinely care about one another. The result is a personality detached from its own sense of aliveness, forced to imitate personal exchanges rather than experience them, much like Bach's man, who can simulate a machine. Close acquaintance with a pathological or malignant narcissist also imposes contrivance on any personality who finds themselves enfolded within the narcissist's world; in order to create safety and belonging for oneself, suppression of voice and selfhood is required, placing one in the position of attempting to accommodate the narcissist's mercurial dictates and sensibilities. Spontaneity, uniqueness, and playfulness all face compromise. Instead, the violated self is dominated by hypervigilance, by rehearsal, and by careful orchestration of their responses.

Like Shaw, I see malignant narcissism as a derivative of repeated relational trauma that likely unfolds over the course of one's childhood. I also conceive of malignant narcissism as a traumatizing state in which the very selfhood of the other faces compromise, murderous degradation, and effective spiritual rape. Central to this formulation is a view of "self" as being a foundational construct essential to any understanding of both subjectivity and intersubjectivity. As a result of being traumatized by a malignant narcissist, I would say that the self becomes compressed into an ever-smaller space, progressively becoming more distorted and emaciated and progressively more agonized and pain-ridden. And, finally, like Daniel Shaw, I would say that the effects of such trauma readily extend throughout a lifetime, deeply coloring the way one relates to oneself and to others. Like Kernberg, I see malignant narcissism as a confluence of pathological narcissism, antisocial behavior, paranoia, and spiteful aggression (sadism).

I also see it as a unitary concept whose core dynamics all flow from a single entity. Antisocial behavior, paranoia, and spiteful aggression would all seem to extend from the core characteristics of pathological narcissism Diamond et al. (2022) identify (as mentioned earlier) exploitativeness, self-centeredness, entitlement, and interpersonal antagonism. Indeed, the Diamond group confirm that they see pathological narcissism as unfolding on a continuum, as I do.

The DSM-5 implicitly recognizes that narcissism may wear many guises, demonstrating both quantitative and qualitative differences between its various forms dependent upon how many of a cluster of nine symptoms a given individual demonstrates (a minimum of five are required).

My presumption – and it's perhaps a significant leap of faith – is that the kind of traumatizing impact that the malignant narcissist inflicts upon those people that he targets likely represents, in exaggerated form, dynamics and processes that inform the nature of trauma that people diagnosed with NPD impose on others. While I see quantitative differences that distinguish the traumatic effects of various forms of pathological narcissism, including malignant narcissism at the extreme end of the scale, I also recognize that as our understanding of trauma associated with pathological narcissism deepens, we may recognize qualitative differences in the nature of trauma targeted individuals endure that corresponds to particular forms of narcissism we're able to discern with the benefit of future knowledge. The position I have adopted is informed by the extensive clinical work that I have undertaken with individuals who have been injured by others who could be described either as Narcissistic Personality Disorders or as malignant narcissists. Other than my clinical data, however, I do not have other data that would substantiate the assumption that I have made. I am not aware of research data that would bear upon this question. There are, however, other clinical opinions (like Diamond et al., 2022) that support the continuum conception. Elder (1986) comments that Steiner (1982) also made explicit his belief that the malignancy of narcissistic, destructive organization unfolds on a continuum, a position that she believed several other analysts implicitly endorsed.

It must also be true that the level and nature of injury people sustain in a narcissistic surround will be reflective of the unique qualities and array of assets/vulnerabilities that define them as individuals and that are likely to arise out of the constitutional givens that characterize them. In that sense, of course, one would expect to see qualitative differences in the way that people respond to the injuries that their relationship with a traumatizing narcissist might cause them. However, my supposition is that the destructive dynamics that characterize various levels of pathological narcissism will vary largely by degree rather than kind. This supposition seems particularly likely to be true if narcissistic personality disorder and malignant narcissism that flow from healthy narcissistic states through to extremely pathological ones are all part of the same continuum. In such a context, malignant narcissism would of necessity need to be a unitary concept; if it is not and is instead an intersection of several different personality disorders, then one would expect to see qualitative differences in the destructive impact of different forms of narcissism.

I clearly see malignant narcissism as a unitary entity that quite naturally extends itself from other pathological forms of narcissism, but others hold different views about this issue. Before the questions I have raised can be resolved satisfactorily, more research and more clinical observation will be required. I merely state my position and my assumptions so that the reader is aware of them and so that the reader can struggle with some of these distinctions themselves, participating in the search for answers that we have yet to satisfactorily acquire. Further complicating the matter, we do recognize that narcissistic personality disorder can, indeed, co-occur with other forms of disorders, including "suicide (Ronningstam, Weinberg, and Maltsberger, 2008), comorbid psychiatric conditions (Stinson, Dawson, Goldstein, Chou, Huang et al., 2008), interpersonal relationship problems (Ogrodniczuk et al., 2009) and emotional distress and functional impairment (Miller, Campbell, and Pilkonis, 2007)" (see Kealy & Ogrudniczuk, 2014, p. 104). In such a context, can one still expect to see the same core dynamics that seem to define narcissism playing themselves out in much the same form or would the shape of narcissistic dynamics then likely change both quantitatively and qualitatively? The closer one looks, the more complex the questions and the interactions that one has to weigh become; in part, for ease of discussion, I will focus upon what I understand to be known about pathological narcissism, trying as carefully and as accurately as I can to outline what I believe narcissism's core dynamics look like.

I would now like to move on to a more detailed description of the injuries that I see people having to struggle within the context of an ongoing relationship with narcissistic others. I regard these people as being closely acquainted with that group of patients who could be described as largely or predominantly VN:

> Consider, now, the nature of attachment that unfolds in a relationship with the narcissistic other. Uniqueness is shuttered. The self is called upon to orchestrate itself, simulating a presence it vainly attempts to contrive to appease the other whose moods and perspectives seem to fluctuate arbitrarily. And the self is given to understand it must negate itself and render itself invisible so that it can be receptive to the narcissistic voice, which expects to still the voices of those around it. Internal richness is forfeit; so, too, are opportunities to expand the self and enhance identity. Safety and resilience are, in the main, compromised; instead, the self is largely defined by its desperate and often covert attempts to survive its own desolation. The self is denied value and is denied the opportunity to feel and give love, which the narcissist would find unbearable. Instead, as the self is subjected to repeated assaults and acts of cruelty, its capacity to experience a broad range of emotions becomes blunted; in their place, shame, vindictive rage, and envy flourish. Shame arises from a sense of the self as defenseless and ineffectual, unable to protect itself in the face of incessant violation. It asserts itself because the self feels unworthy of the other's love (your failure to love me confirms my defectiveness). And it is experienced because the self increasingly recognizes that it is skeletal and emaciated. The self's inadequacies and distortions feel agonizingly transparent; transparency further exacerbates the exquisitely painful levels of vulnerability the self must live with. Perpetual, unrelenting vigilance ensues. In spite of its best efforts to hide vulnerability, its struggle is all too readily apparent to the surrounding world, marking it for predation (bullying).

With the passage of time and the accumulation of disturbing, monstrous, vindictive feelings, shame becomes particularly acute and particularly private. No one must see the horrific realities inside. An individual so affected looks greedily at those around him or her who seem to be more complete or more gracious. Depth of attachment becomes ever more untenable; dissociation, contrivance, and an indelible sense of one's own unattractiveness render the possibility of ever becoming an accepted or even esteemed member of the human community seem increasingly remote. Depression flourishes, imposing its own attendant consequences that further subvert personal value, exacerbate depletion and emaciation, and erode whatever shards of hope remained that one can construct a life of one's own. Thinking about suicide offers avenues of escape in an otherwise impossibly bleak landscape; so, also, does avoidant behavior (including addictions) that is relied upon to provide momentary relief from unbearable suffering, but which only intensifies personal inadequacy arising from compromised productivity. And, finally, set upon by a surrounding world and an internal one that both assume an increasingly malignant aspect, the self endlessly tries to prepare itself for expected new incursions through perpetual rehearsals of responses to worst-case scenarios that, tragically, it is rarely able to consummate. This form of anxiety disorder – what is now conceptually being referred to as complex posttraumatic stress disorder (PTSD) – becomes an early friend and ofttimes lifelong companion for those who endured narcissistic invasions in their childhoods.

In the face of all its burdens, the self becomes preoccupied with annihilation – both literal and psychological" (Wood, 2023, pp. 171–172).

At the very center of the dynamics informing the injuries one sustains in a narcissistic surround is an emaciated, depleted self. A sense of feeling shamefully and transparently incomplete dominates one's subjectivity. The emergent self feels painfully defenseless and terribly ill-equipped to manage in the world, at one and the same time impossibly hungry for relationships and terrified that the self can all too easily be overwhelmed by other personalities. Simultaneously, the self is excruciatingly aware of the ease with which it can be wounded, subject to buffeting emotions that disorder it and intensify its public vulnerability. This conception of the injured self is most compatible with a Kohutian view of the self as damaged and as deficient, hungry for repair but desperately afraid to seek out help for fear of further violation. It stands in contrast to the rigidly organized, pathological self-system one has come to recognize as demarcating narcissistic states built around deeply and rigidly entrenched grandiosity.

As has been seen in the foregoing section, some of the literature on VN suggests that underneath the exquisite vulnerability that the vulnerable narcissist experiences lies a grandiose core marked by perfectionistic strivings and expectations/aspirations for larger-than-life successes. I would counter that people targeted by narcissistic personalities have often been nearly continuously confronted by invidious comparisons that repeatedly emphasize their shortfalls relative to the narcissistic other. As a consequence, they have internalized a core message that the narcissist conveys: "if you're not me, if you don't meet my standards, you're shit." Perception of their own emaciation and inadequacy consolidates their despair and their shame, but does not relieve them of their toxic expectations. Their "grandiosity," such as it is, informs their agony rather than allowing them to stand apart from others and consolidate self-esteem around an omnipotent self. It connotes a terrible absence that they must contend with: in metaphor, their subjective "failure" to become a full person possessed of definable agency and voice. I very much agree with Daniel Shaw: the therapeutic task is to create an environment in which healthy aspirational striving can be expressed and can begin to be fulfilled. Again, calling upon both Shaw and Kohut, I see their underlying grandiosity as fragments or a residue of what might otherwise have been a healthy narcissistic yearning to make the most of oneself and to extend one's uniqueness into some sort of fulfilling productivity. Grandiose strivings additionally capture the introjected expectations of the narcissistic other paired with a double-bind message: "if you don't meet my impossible standards, you're unworthy of my respect and my love, but if you attempt to consummate whatever talent and uniqueness you possess, I will punish you."

Some of the research on VN, previously reviewed, has suggested that such patients are masochistic, are resistant to treatment, and glory in their suffering, having developed fixed, elaborate narratives of victimhood that enhance grandiosity by defeating a therapist's attempts to help them. I see such people as having been compelled to strike a bargain between how much selfhood they can consummate and how much they must suppress in order to create safety for themselves. The internalized persecutor is ever watchful, prepared to "attack" whenever the self enjoys too much expansion and even when it becomes too ambitious and too self-interested. The self has internalized the narcissistic voice in part so that it can anticipate when the narcissistic other is likely to scald it with excoriating shame and humiliation, if not outright assault. In this manner, the "masochism" that one observes in such vulnerable people is self-protective but also, of course, terribly self-limiting. The hypervigilance that attends this dynamic may all too soon lay the foundations for complex PTSD experiences (another propositional diagnosis that, it would probably be fair to say, has gained considerable credibility amongst practitioners, having been incorporated into the psychodynamic diagnostic manual – 2). "Complex" has been added to the diagnostic entity because it is believed that the emergence of PTSD process during critical developmental years disrupts foundational maturational striving.

So, what does cPTSD look like as it begins to manifest itself? Hypervigilance produces incessant, relentless fear rehearsal, consideration of worst-case scenarios that one could face with the narcissistic other, the self then rehearses endlessly in an attempt to sidestep disastrous consequences. Remember that the self feels terribly precarious and terribly ephemeral, informed by a sense that further injuries can utterly compromise and annihilate it. Annihilation of the self is a profoundly and relentlessly held preoccupation. Among the patients that I have worked with, cPTSD does not consistently emerge, but it does so with alarming frequency, further intensifying suffering and, not inconsequentially, also further compromising functioning, which has the effect of further limiting the self's options. Those patients whom I have worked with who rely heavily on repressive defenses seem more poorly equipped to articulate the self's struggles for survival, effectively inoculating them, at least to some degree, from cPTSD retraumatization, but at a cost: it becomes harder for them to appreciate the nature of the trauma that they have endured and the nature of the conflicts that they face with themselves and with others. Those people for whom agonies associated with annihilatory experiences are more prominently recognized seem to be more likely to develop debilitating cPTSD symptomatology, but they are also relatively advantaged in the self-exploration that they undertake.

In both groups – for simplicity's sake, the repressive and nonrepressive groups – one sees considerable curtailment of potentiality. Oftentimes, people are acutely aware that somehow they're getting in their own way and obstructing their own possibilities. They can see that they might be more than they are, assailing themselves for their shortfalls and/or desperate to escape the terrible constriction that defines the self, but nonetheless are too afraid to extend themselves. Paradoxically, for some of these patients, at least, it may require considerable work for them to recognize just how frightened they are of expanding the self; for others, the nature of their fear is very declarative. It is typically critical to help them recognize the intensity of terror that "growing" can induce in them. Contrary to the portrait that has been painted of VN individuals, a significant portion of them – at least in my clinical work – managed to break free and transcend the self-negation that has defined them, becoming perhaps not all that they might hope for themselves but a substantial part of the person that they wanted to express. Unconscious acts of self-sabotage could persist, but in abated form. For others, self-negation continues to obstruct their lives, denying them the opportunity to be productively self-interested in their work and in their love lives. The therapeutic task then shifts towards helping them mitigate the depression that an awareness of their limitations creates for them. This work becomes particularly poignant when one is dealing with individuals who are clearly quite talented, but for whom the expression of such talent feels too dangerous to realize. Understandably, that discrepancy can be torturous.

I would say that everyone in this group of patients remains cognizant that they do not feel entirely safe in the world, but, especially for those who make substantial progress in expressing their talent, concern about safety is no longer quite as acutely felt.

At this point, it is probably timely to focus upon the compromises such a self makes in its relationship choices. Because the self feels so emaciated, it is quite desperate to obtain sustenance. Because it feels so inadequate and so embarrassingly incomplete, it experiences itself as profoundly unattractive. As described earlier, it is also deeply afraid that others can harm it and, at the same time, that it lacks the strength to navigate its way through life's challenges. Quite a complicated brew of contrasting needs. Its realities compel compromise in its relationship choices that only further extend its trauma. If the self feels sufficiently unsafe in the world, it may choose a narcissistic other as a partner, sheltering under the "strength" that the narcissistic personality proffers, only to face further diminishment and shaming and deepening concerns about personal annihilation. Envy and excoriation coming from both self and the other amplify themselves. Caught in such a relationship and pervaded by both fear and hunger, the self may offer itself up for diminishment and abnegation as a means of appeasing the narcissistic other who has to endure the self's terrible shortfalls. The need for someone – anyone – to fill the empty spaces inside is disturbingly compelling, particularly in the absence of a sense that one can manage in the world by oneself.

Other compromises also present themselves. The damaged self may choose other people who are either similarly damaged or whose damage eclipses their own. In this context, the self is able to undercut and side-step its own fears of abandonment because the other is even more deeply preoccupied with abandonment than they are. Taking care of the other and attending to their fears allows the self to vicariously address its own needs in relatively greater safety. In this context, the self can experience itself, however faultily, as enjoying a modestly expanded sense of power and authority that might quickly collapse in the absence of the other ("your dependence and your neediness makes me feel bigger").

Or the damaged self may choose someone who is relatively inert emotionally who has demonstrated themselves able to navigate their way through the practical challenges of life with relative ease. This compromise must eventually accentuate starvation, but it also affirms place and belonging inasmuch as the self is possessed of gifts (its emotional sensitivities) that the other lacks.

And finally – this short list of alternatives is not meant to represent an exhaustive compendium – unbearable emaciation and starvation may compel the self to allow another personality to displace it, filling it with someone else's prerogatives, needs, sensibilities, perspectives, values, etc. The resulting death of self promises rebirth in a new, but alien form. Sometimes, this means that the self becomes that which it may both abhor and fear – the narcissistic other.

Very occasionally, I should add, I see people who have been significantly violated by narcissistic others who make positive relationship choices – that is, relationship choices that enhance their opportunities for growth and for the development of voice and personhood. People able to do so seem to be people in my practice who had access to a parent who could effectively oppose the narcissistic presence of the other parent.

In my experience, these various relationship manifestations may all express themselves in the transference or, if one likes, in the shape of relationship that the patient establishes in his\her work with the therapist.

There are other costs to narcissistic predation that need to be considered. Depression is certainly one of them. People possessed of a withered or skeletal self feel profoundly depleted, robbed of much hope for the future and, therefore, purpose. They find it hard both to imagine and to construct a place for themselves in the human community. Relationship choices informed by trauma further accentuate depletion; so also do endemic levels of fear that, alongside depression, generate terrible cognitive inefficiencies that further compromise an already impaired capacity for productivity. Depression is further amplified by people's relative inability to identify life passions that derive from an authentic self. In consequence of all of these considerations and probably others that I have failed to mention, the self faces an ongoing struggle with depletion. The more energy that the self devotes towards a desired goal, the more the self feels like it's running out of gas; sustaining effort and concentration is profoundly difficult. The more energy the self expends, the more depleted it feels, and the more depleted it feels, the more its exposure to incipient depression grows. As an aside, this is often an unconscious process that needs to be articulated in therapy work. In response to growing depression, the self seeks out diversionary or escapist activities that generate momentary pleasure, but serve to distract it from the crucial work it is trying to undertake. Escapist activities can include addictive behaviors (gambling, sexual addictions) and substance abuse, further exacerbating concerns about worthlessness and competence. Repeated, strong suicidal preoccupations that may extend over the course of years during the treatment process often present themselves.

Because the self is denied the opportunity to enhance its uniqueness and craft a voice that grows out of its own genuine prerogatives, interests, and values, it is denied the opportunity to hear the music that informs normal human social intercourse – the fun, spontaneity, playfulness, creativity, inventiveness, humor, generosity, and openness to others, as a short list – that allows one to feel real and that helps one to feel that the relationships one is participating in, including the relationship with oneself, are immersive and rewarding. The emaciated self is instead forced to contrive a presence, simulating its humanity so that it can be presentable to others and can feign interaction with them. Empty, exhausting social interchanges ensue; the self eventually desires a safe place where it can retreat so it can be spared the effort of having to "fake" it yet again. The absence of human sustenance, which it might otherwise obtain for itself were it capable of feeling and of being more real only enhances the pervasive dissociation that it has relied upon to numb the effects of the trauma that it has endured.

Envy and its close companion rage distort the inner world of the targeted individual, filling it with retaliatory, murderous fantasies that render their inner life a very dangerous, dark, ugly vista. Mistrust and paranoia elaborate themselves. Fighting back can mean annihilation; failure to fight back traps one in helpless rage and despair that only compounds itself. For those people that do find the means to vigorously oppose the narcissistic voice and narcissistic needs, there is the danger that they, too, can build safety around a retaliatory presence of their own, replicating the narcissistic voice in their later adult relationships. Those that don't may experience progressive dying of the self that only amplifies itself as their life unfolds. For many people who have been repeatedly targeted by narcissistic rapacity, their own too-close acquaintance with the growing darkness inside generates indelible fears about the "monster" they carry within. Helping people recognize such fear is oft-times an uneasy undertaking, but one that, if accomplished, offers people a significant measure of relief. The monster is still there, but it doesn't feel quite as formidable or as dangerous, though, to be fair, still discon-certingly close to the surface at times. Clearly, exploring this aspect of people's psyches must be carried out with great respect and sensitiv-ity. Monster-inside feelings can sometimes contribute to intense suicidal experiences, but looking into this arena of phenomenology can also be dangerously disorganizing whenever doors are opened.

The compilation of starvation, contrivance, dissociation, and in-ner darkness all contribute to an experience of deadness. It becomes hard to feel anything but negative self-states like numbness, fear, rage, envy, and retaliation. In an attempt to relieve the pervasive but often poorly understood pain that such inner deadness creates, the self may, like the narcissistic other, tend to act out cruelty and sadism to create a momentary sense of aliveness. Doing so only enhances hopelessness and the conviction that one is profoundly bad. Exploration of cruelty often represents an attempt on the part of the self to try to capture what it is that makes living things animate.

I summarized some of the costs that I have just described in this passage in my book:

> The narcissist replicates many of the conditions that define his own inner life – starvation; enduring, suffocating hunger; envy of all that others appear to have that the self is missing; fear of depend-ence; contrivance; a taste for cruelty; a blighted rage filled interior; a profound sense of inner badness; a sense that one's inner and external worlds are infiltrated by threat and malevolence; and high levels of vigilance. (pp. 177–178)

The portrait I have painted confirms, for me, the traumatizing nar-cissist's unconscious predilection to re-create much of the distortion that characterizes his inner life and the inner lives of the people he violates. Now, I would draw attention to some of the imposing differ-ences that appear to divide these two groups of people – GN and VN. I will again cite a passage from my original book:

> Unlike a narcissistic personality, shame is a prominent experience (among patients who endure narcissistic violation). So, too, is fear of abandonment, depression, subjectively high levels of self-hatred, inertia, and ruminative equivocation. And, unlike the narcissist,

rather than feeling the need to occupy center stage continuously, there is a strong drive to disappear and erase oneself that includes a need to back away from successes and disconfirm them. Sense of inner badness and of one's own attractiveness is exquisitely apparent whereas in the narcissist it is hidden. The self is also experienced as helpless and powerless as opposed to being infected with grandiosity and indomitability. Healthy entitlement is damaged and certainly not inflated in the way that it is in a narcissistic personality. (p. 178)

For me, these differences are crucial. The individual who is being seen as VN, as frightened and as self-protective as they are, has a far greater tolerance for neediness and vulnerability than someone whose personality is rigidly organized around a grandiose self. Their boundaries are far more permeable (often painfully so) and as a consequence they are more open to the impact that other people can have upon them. As much as they are marked by despair and agony, they can still let people inside in a way and to a degree that the pathologically grandiose narcissist cannot. They can still be touched and moved by other people in spite of their crippling fears and, accordingly, many of them can be potentially helped; work may be stormy and hard going, but one has a sense that there is another person present in the relationship who can at least intermittently experience genuine contact with themselves and with others in a healing environment. They much more readily invoke compassion and empathy that helps to inform the therapist's desire to help. Many such people - at least in my clinical experience – actually prove to be surprisingly easy to collaborate with, readily establishing a very productive working relationship and a productive interdependence that has sometimes taken me aback. The greatest hurdles, as I have seen them, are to be faced when patients attempt to transition treatment relationship gains into the world outside therapy. Taking risks in the real interpersonal world can be fraught with substantial dangers, including temporary regression into psychotic states or acutely suicidal states when risks that people take in their relationships catastrophically re-expose them to trauma. Even people who have realized considerable treatment success can find themselves subject to what I call regression to an earlier ego state – situations in which a traumatic life challenge re-immerses them in the helpless, frightened, skeletal persona that once defined them. Such regressions are also capable of generating striking disruptions in people's lives, including relationship compromise and intense suicidal feelings. Both the nature of vulnerability that such people endure and the intense regression to earlier ego state experiences that periodically invade them stand in striking contrast to the rageful invulnerability of both the pathological and malignant narcissist.

To reiterate for clarification, much like Shaw, people being designated as VN in the literature are people that I see as having been violated by grandiose narcissists.

The lines between narcissists and the people they have exploited can become difficult to discern, however, as one looks at higher functioning narcissistic personalities (often very successful people) versus vulnerable, targeted individuals who are functioning at low borderline levels. In these circumstances, therapeutic effort required with the latter group of people certainly feels more imposing and more chaotic than work with the former; indeed, higher-functioning narcissistic people may demonstrate a capacity for relatedness and a greater tolerance for insight than lower-functioning vulnerable individuals, rendering work with the former more enjoyable and seemingly more productive. On most occasions that I have worked with higher functioning narcissistic individuals, however, the work has frequently felt self-limiting. One wanted to go deeper, but somehow it proved to be tantalizingly difficult to get there. In contrast, working with people at a vulnerable borderline level overwhelmed one with the depth of material that one was confronting; the task of bringing it together in helping them construct a coherent self was what was so hard.

Clearly, the conceptual frameworks that I'm attempting to build – much like the frameworks that others have constructed – are challenging to apply in the real clinical world populated by immensely complex personalities. While I and others I have referenced made this point earlier in this book, I think it is important to reiterate how approximate some of our work and some of our models are.

Having reemphasized this point, I want to return to the topic of malignant narcissism. I see it as an extreme form of narcissism and as part of a narcissistic continuum because I think narcissism – or at least pathological narcissism – represents a continuum demarcated by an increasing turning away from relatedness, interconnection, and interdependence towards investment in an increasingly pathological self-state (much like Kernberg) – one in which a narcissistic personality insulates itself to an ever greater degree from the impact of others' voices and personalities. Its function is to shut other people out and, as individuals become more and more narcissistic, to eradicate and deconstruct the other so that one can sidestep bonds of attachment and love. Narcissistic solipsism can never form an unbreachable wall; defenses must always be flawed, particularly when they are directed toward our profound and abiding need for human connection. Subjectively, however, the malignant narcissist creates a strong impression of being impervious to foundational human realities like our need to touch one another in the variety of ways that we do.

Narcissistic dedication to disabling others' creativity and authority (save for those facets of others' productivity they can harness for transactional ends) also highlights another important aspect of the narcissistic continuum: increasing investment in devitalization and deadness and a turning away from life-giving activity. Rather than enhancing others' aliveness by enabling them to expand their sense of self and express their unique qualities, the pathological narcissist draws away the literal selfhood of the other, filling the other with, for him, a desirable version of himself. It is for this reason I suggested in my previous book that I think narcissistic personalities gave rise to the vampire legend: a seeming monster half alive and half dead who draws the life out of those around him in a hopeless attempt to create an illusion of life and of satiety for himself.

Within the framework of this formulation, the transition between vulnerability and grandiosity becomes more meaningful. As an individual becomes decisively committed to organizing their personality around grandiosity (what could be described as a predominantly GN position) they have undertaken an enormously important qualitative shift, sacrificing their potential for humanity so that they might protect themselves by establishing imperviousness to human need. In contrast, people who have been repeatedly violated by pathologically narcissistic personalities remain, in the main, organized around vulnerability, thereby relatively protecting their potentiality for life and growth, though at the cost of great personal suffering. Choosing one path (predominant grandiosity) or the other (predominant vulnerability) does not unfold with full awareness of what is happening to the self; for most people, "choice" is a misnomer, implying that they are in charge of destiny that trauma has played a major role in shaping. Subjectively, however, one can imagine that the allure of grandiosity makes it feel like not only a necessary but a desirable course to set for the self.

As I noted in my book on malignant narcissism, I can imagine circumstances in which narcissistic predation may compel one to adopt a grandiose version of narcissism, eschewing vulnerability and pain in exchange for a toxic version of strength and power. In a context in which the violated individual is given to understand that emulation of the narcissistic other is not only desirable, but necessary for survival, I can foresee such an identification unfolding, particularly in the absence of a protective parental other who can mitigate the narcissistic voice. In the absence of such protection, the targeted individual faces impossible contingencies: either identify with the aggressor and imitate their destructiveness or face personal annihilation. If the targeted individual is possessed of dispositional or congenital givens that equip them to make such an accommodation, they can consolidate a self around grandiosity; if they are not so equipped, one can imagine that they would face failure, derision, and shaming. The narcissistic personality could be expected to experience their child's "weakness" as a source of deep personal compromise. In his attempt to disavow such weakness in himself, the narcissistic parent could be seen to redouble his efforts to destroy his recalcitrant surrogate. The successful child, on the other hand, is never entirely relieved of the sense of threat that they experience. Safety can only be acquired if they can color between the lines, imitating their narcissistic parent and enacting his prerogatives, but never doing so in a way that advances the importance of their voice over that of their mentor.

Something like this happens on a societal level as well. A malignantly narcissistic leader appeals to disaffected members of his nation or culture, promising to heal wounds occasioned by economic reversals, war, dispossession, threats to cultural sensibilities, immigration, etc., that undercut integrity, safety, and dignity. Those that identify with him and with the prerogatives of power that his grandiosity seductively offers are treated with favor, but only if they enact his prerogatives. They can bask in the shared grandiosity that they have acquired from a powerful other. Those who maintain individuality and a voice of their own face excoriation and annihilation.

Newly minted acolytes can fill themselves with their newly inflated sense of power, but they do so having surrendered their most human parts to forge a new identity – their capacity for fallibility, interdependence, need, generativity, and humility. Relationships are shaped by hierarchies of power rather than personal connections. Like the malignant narcissist, they, too, begin to starve, denied the sustenance and the meaning that respectful interconnectivity can generate. As this dying takes place, they become more receptive to the narcissistic leader's enticement to fill themselves with the pleasures of cruelty and dominance.

Increasingly, they can only simulate aliveness rather than feel it; acts of brutality allow them to at least feel something. There is another powerful reason that cruelty becomes so compelling for them: they live in a fear-drenched world defined by the malignant narcissist's wandering hatreds. No one can feel safe. Safety is achieved through acts of debasement directed towards identified outliers and enemies. Fear is simultaneously assuaged and inflamed as one's ability to hurt and diminish others is repeatedly confirmed. Cruelty is rationalized as an extension of a larger national purpose – usually the acquisition of strength and power at others' expense. In this closed, upside-down world, morality is measured by conquest and rapacity. Just as the malignant narcissist has placed himself on a continuous war footing, so must his subjects. Falling inside the boundaries of his world marks one as good; falling on the outside marks one as other and as contemptible. Part of the insidious bargain that a subject strikes with the narcissistic other entails an implicit promise that the narcissistic leader will shelter his follower from his rage only if the latter becomes what the narcissist requires of him.

Both Kernberg and Kohut (1969–70) alongside numbers of other authors (see, for example, Fromm, 1964; Hughes, 2018, 2019; Mika, 2017; Padilla et al., 2007) recognized the immense power of group regression in the face of perceived social threat and in response to malignant narcissistic leadership:

> Under conditions of social upheaval, turmoil or stress and in the presence of a powerful paranoid leadership, the group (can shift) into the opposite extreme of endorsing a primitive, powerful, sadistic leader who will assure the group that, by identifying collectively with the threatening primitive aggression he incorporates, they will be safe from persecution by becoming persecutors themselves.
>
> (Kernberg, 1989, p. 202)

And:

> (Kohut) foresaw that the individual who had endured narcissistic injury themselves might "seek to melt into the body of a powerful nation (as symbolized by a grandiose leader) to cure their shame and provide them with the feeling of enormous strength, to which they react with relief and triumph (Kohut's essay "On Leadership" cited in my book, *A Study of Malignant Narcissism*, p. 24). Several pages later in his leadership essay Kohut went on to add "The most

malignant human propensities are mobilized in support of national-
istic narcissistic rage."

(Wood, 2023, p. 24)

I have argued that the dynamic forces that characterize malignant
narcissism and more extreme forms of pathological narcissism are to
be found unfolding, albeit in attenuated form, throughout the continuum of narcissistic disorders. I do recognize, again, that this is an enor-
mous assumption to make. It has to be tested and retested by further
clinical observation and further research. This is only the beginning
of the conversation, even though this conversation has been unfolding for over 100 years. Other clinicians will add their voices and their
formulations and introduce their evidence. Eventually, we'll get ourselves to a better, more coherent place, realizing a more profound and
thoroughgoing understanding of narcissistic processes. Both healthy
and pathological forms of narcissism appear to play a critical role in
our continuously unfolding human story – hence the urgency to know
them better.

In the next chapter, I would like to tie some of the relational conceptions of both traumatizing narcissists and the people that they violate
to clinical examples that I hope will successfully elucidate ideas I have
just described. I will draw heavily upon clinical examples that Daniel
Shaw has provided in his book, *Traumatizing Narcissism*, as well as review some of my own patient work. Because I am not comfortable providing portraits of patients' lives – fearing that they might recognize
themselves – I can offer descriptions of the kind of themes and issues
that I have encountered with people who grew up in what I understood
to be an injurious narcissistic surround.

References

Bach, S. (1975). Narcissism, continuity and the uncanny. *The International
Journal of Psychoanalysis*, *56*, 77–86.

Bach, S., & Schwartz, L. (1972). A dream of the Marquis de Sade. *Journal of
the American Psychoanalytic Association*, *20*, 451–475.

Berke, J. (1985). Envy loveth not: A study of the origin, influence, and confluence of envy and narcissism. *British Journal of Psychotherapy*, *1*(3),
171–186.

Diamond, D., Yeomans, F. E., Stern, B. L., & Kernberg O. F. (2022). *Treating pathological narcissism with transference-focused psychotherapy*. The
Guilford Press.

Elder, P. (1986). Kleinian developments in the concept of narcissism. *British Journal of Psychotherapy, 3*(1), 65–71.

Fromm, E. (1964). *The heart of man.* Harper and Row.

Howell, E. (2005). *The dissociative mind.* Routledge.

Hughes, I. (2018). *Disordered minds: How dangerous personalities are destroying democracy.* Zero Books.

Hughes, I. (2019). Disordered minds: Democracy as a defense against dangerous personalities. In B. Lee (Ed.), *The dangerous case of Donald Trump* (2nd ed., pp. 446–457). Thomas Dunne Books.

Kalsched, D. E. (1996). *The inner world of trauma: Archetypical defenses of the personal spirit.* Routledge.

Kealy, D., & Ogrodniczuk, J. (2014). Pathological narcissism and the obstruction of love. *Psychodynamic Psychiatry, 42*(1), 101–119.

Kernberg, O. (1989). The temptations off conventionality. *The International Review of Psychoanalysis, 18*, 191–204.

Kohut, H. (1969–70). On leadership. In P. H. Ornstein (Ed.), *The search for the self* (Vol. 3, pp. 103–128). Routledge.

Mika, E. (2017). Who goes Trump? Tyranny as a triumph of narcissism. In B. Lee (Ed.), *The dangerous case of Donald Trump* (2nd ed., pp. 289–308). Thomas Dunne Books.

Miller, J. D., Campbell, W. K., & Pilkonis, P. A. (2007). Narcissistic personality disorder: Relations with distress and functional impairment. *Comprehensive Psychiatry, 48*, 170–177.

Ogrudniczuk, J. S., Piper, W. E., Joyce, A. S., Steinberg, P. I., & Duggal, S. (2009). Interpersonal problems associated with narcissism among psychiatric outpatients. *Journal of Psychiatric Research*, 43, 837–842.

Padilla, A., Hogan, R., & Kaiser, R. B. (2007). The toxic triangle: Destructive leaders, susceptible followers, and conducive followers. *Leadership Quarterly, 18*, 176–194.

Ronningstam, E., Weinberg, I., & Maltsberger, J. T. (2008). Eleven deaths of Mr. K.: Contributing factors to suicide in narcissistic personalities. *Psychiatry: Interpersonal and Biological Processes. 71*(2), 169–182.

Shaw, D. (2010). Enter ghosts: The loss of intersubjectivity in clinical work with adult children of pathological narcissists. *Psychoanalytic Dialogues, 20*, 46–59.

Shaw, D. (2014). *Traumatic narcissism: Relational systems of subjugation.* Routledge.

Shengold, L. (1989). *Soul murder: The effects of childhood abuse and deprivation.* Fawcett.

Spitz, R. A. (1963). Life and the dialogue. In H. S. Gaskill (Ed.), *Counterpoint: Libidinal object and subject.* International Universities Press.

Steiner, J. (1982). Perverse relationships between parts of the self. *International Journal of Psychoanalysis, 62*, 241–251.

Stinson, F. S., Dawson, D. A., Goldstein, R. B., Chou, S. P., Huang, B., Smith, S. M., Ruan, W. J., Pulay, A. J., Saha, T. D., Pickering, R. P., & Grant, B. F. (2008). Prevalence, correlates, disability, and co-morbidity of DSM-IV narcissistic personality disorder: Results from the wave 2 national epidemiological survey on alcohol and related conditions. *Journal of Clinical Psychiatry*, 69, 1033–1045.

Wood, R. (2023). *A study of malignant narcissism: Personal and professional insights*. Routledge.

Chapter 5

Additional Clinical Examples

The first patient of Daniel Shaw's that I want to review is a man in his 40s with two children who, overall, seems to be functioning at a relatively high level and who, in therapy, seems largely capable of a successful collaboration with his analyst. The analytic relationship, at least as it is described, does not appear to have been marked by stark, abrupt ruptures disconcerting to both patient and therapist; instead, Shaw's patient, who is designated as "Tom," works more or less productively in therapy save for persistent dissociative states that oftentimes render it difficult for Tom to recall some of the core themes and feelings that have emerged in the therapeutic work.

Tom's relational system, as Shaw would name it, seems to have consisted of both a narcissistic mother and father. Mother was described as being intolerant of any view or perspective that differed from her own as, indeed, it sounded like father was as well. The offense that mother and father presented Tom should he attempt to stand by his own appreciation of a given experience was sharply expressed: father would be upset with Tom for having distressed his mother and, in turn, adopted a posture of victimization should Tom attempt to talk about what the relationship with father felt like. Asserting himself and drawing clear boundaries felt so imposing for Tom that he likened it to facing Mount Everest. As Tom admitted to himself, it felt safer to not say anything and find a place where he could retreat that offered him a measure of peace. He unconsciously gave voice to what he imagined others' experiences and preferences were rather than talking about his own feelings and needs. In effect, he allowed others' wishes to define him rather than recognize and act on his own desires. In this sense, as Shaw said, he became an object in his own life that others acted upon rather than a subject

DOI: 10.4324/9781032649535-5

who authored the events in his life in a way that was consonant with a real self. With the support of analytic work, he began to be able to acknowledge that creating a real self and using his own voice was both guilt-inducing and shameful for him; guilt was sufficiently intense, Shaw believed, that it often obscured Tom's anger and the urgency of his desire to make enough space for a self that belonged to him.

Shaw poignantly captured the dilemma facing Tom. Dealing with parents who were traumatizing narcissists meant that Tom was attempting to negotiate a self with people for whom "the subjectivity of the other is a threat to (their) sense of superiority" (p. 92). The traumatizing narcissist "is unwilling to acknowledge insufficiency of any kind, unwilling to be accountable or contrite, unwilling to atone, and sees no reason to ask for any kind of forgiveness" (p. 92). How, then, Shaw wondered, could Tom expect to realize the acknowledgment from his parents that Tom imagined was necessary for him to free himself from their grasp? Shaw commented that "hopeless, they fear that they will have to remain stuck where they are, ferrying back and forth between both sides of their ambivalence, loving then hating; other blaming then self blaming; needing connection then needing aloneness; loving aloneness, then hating aloneness, and often just trying to find a way to be numb" (p. 92). As already noted in the preceding chapter, Shaw underscored that therapy with people like Tom unfolded slowly, taking perhaps more time than a therapist might anticipate it would, as people begin to gradually disentangle themselves from their imposing fear of constructing an authentic self. In Tom's case, the work that he had to do with himself would necessitate changing the nature of his relationship with his wife, which, in some respects at least, recapitulated his struggle with his parents. The emergence of grandiose fantasies in the later stages of treatment, Shaw believed, often forecast consummation of significant relational changes. Grandiose fantasies were seen to represent the assertion or reassertion of core wishes, ambitions, and desires that the narcissistic other had suppressed. Beginning to recognize them and act on them was inherently quite a frightening undertaking, implying, as it must, that one was willing to endure and could survive fundamental changes in their core relationships.

My understanding was that Tom did begin to enjoy significant, meaningful progress through his analytic work. Shaw saw analytic work as providing Tom with an experience of intersubjectivity or, if one likes - more simply - relational respect that exposed Tom to a protracted intimacy in which he was encouraged to find and use his own voice.

Shaw references another patient whom he identifies as "Mark." Mark provides a nice example of the potentially healing aspects of the analytic relationship, which, I would say, also captures the healing potential of a relationship that can grow out of psychoanalytic psychotherapy. It seems pertinent to consider Mark's example in the context of the discussion we have just had about the importance of respectful intersubjectivity in therapy.

Mark was described as having grown up with "a powerful, seductive, charming, and subtly domineering father" who found it exceedingly difficult to give up ground, to amend his position, or to acknowledge that he was not right (p. 140). Mark was said to struggle with painful misgivings about his own "power, potency, bigness, and manliness" (p. 139). Mark seemingly played out his deep concerns about dominance and submissiveness through sadomasochistic exchanges with sex workers. As he attempted to exert control over the analyst in the therapeutic context, Shaw emphatically resisted the patient's attempts to control and direct him, turning the patient away in what Shaw later considered was an insensitive and hurtful manner through a heavy-handed interpretation. Years after this exchange, when the patient and therapist refocused their attention on this particular incident, Shaw was able to acknowledge retrospectively he had handled the situation badly and, moreover, genuinely apologize for it. Mark responded quite emotionally, expressing profound relief, telling Shaw how much it meant to him that, unlike his father, Shaw had been able to validate his feelings even though it meant admitting analytic fallibility for Shaw. As testament to the importance of the therapeutic relationship that this repair had helped consolidate, the patient was said to have maintained contact with the therapist over a course of years, sharing pictures and descriptions of various meaningful life events.

Now, I would like to turn my attention toward a third clinical example that Shaw provided, a woman whom he designated "Lorraine." This example highlights for me what one of the core deformations that traumatizing or pathological narcissism occasions: an emaciation of self that renders people hopeless about their capacity to carry on with their lives in their adult years without the "surrogacy" of another traumatizing narcissist who often fills the role of partner or spouse.

Lorraine, like Tom, appears to have been a rather high-functioning individual in her work life, having achieved status as an author and as a tenured professor. Her first partner, Alan, perhaps like her parents, treated her dismissively, diminishing her accomplishments and her contributions. His unflagging sexual desire for her, however, was sufficient to almost irresistibly confirm her value and render him attractive even though mutuality of respect was absent. When Alan unilaterally decided to divorce her, she was gripped with "terror about how unworthy and bad she really was" (p. 87). I think Shaw correctly identified these feelings as a primal, defining childhood pain that enabled him and his patient to better appreciate her most foundational fears. Parenthetically, I have referred to such experience earlier in this book as regression to an earlier ego state, a deeply disconcerting experience in which one is, however, temporarily, reduced to reliving some of the disconcerting horrors of early childhood with a terrible and captivating immediacy. In Lorraine's case, one could guess that her fears were disturbingly tenacious. My view is that a painful sense of emaciation and a deep, almost irresistible conviction in one's utter lack of worth and one's badness is an inevitable consequence of growing up in a narcissistic surround which, by definition, must impose negation of self. Fortunately, Lorraine was possessed of enough resilience to not only survive her divorce, but she seems to have found the means to expand herself in a variety of different important ways, including choosing a partner who was generally capable of making more room for her than Alan had. As this new relationship proved to be too constraining and confining as well, she found the strength to move on, enjoying a sense of optimism and hopefulness about her life that previously would not have been possible for her. Separation no longer filled her with immobilizing horror. Her therapy had made quite a difference for her.

The next and final example that I have drawn from Shaw's book is of a patient (Alice) for whom the injuries occasioned by traumatizing narcissism were so acutely felt and so close to her surface that they disrupted and challenged the therapeutic alliance with great frequency. I cite the example of "Alice" because, unlike the three patients I have just described, transference and countertransference storms were so intense that they repeatedly threatened the viability of the therapeutic work.

Alice was raised by a mother who inflicted nearly continuous narcissistic injury on her in the form of lacerating contempt and distaste and a father who alternated between frightening fits of rage and moments of loving support punctuated by the implication of sexual interference as Alice matured. The contrast between the punishing emotional realities of Alice's home life and the glittering cultural refinement the family presented the outside world as scions of art and psychoanalysis could not have been more sharply drawn.

Alice, I think, is representative of a significant group of people who have been so badly traumatized by pathologically narcissistic others that, as Shaw said:

> the fear of re-traumatization is so persistent that it can become difficult for the analyst to feel effective in any way. Revival of the patient's hopes for recognition creates more vulnerability for the patient that he can tolerate; better to just give up and shut down. Suddenly, the analyst, who thought his/her connection with the patient was growing stronger, is shut out, not to be trusted – just another traumatizer, acting empathic without really being so. (p. 30)

Such people are so wounded, so afraid, and so mistrustful of the world of people around them and, it could be said, so emaciated, so incomplete, and so exquisitely vulnerable that trying to engage in a relationship – even in a "safe" space like psychotherapy or analysis – is very nearly if not virtually untenable. In spite of the therapist's best efforts, he or she is likely to find themselves assailed with patient perception of insensitivity and injuriousness. The nearly unrelenting nature of patient injury readily generates a sense in the therapist/analyst that they, like the patient, are fundamentally bad; in response, the patient inadvertently evokes retaliatory and defensive postures, which make all parties feel even worse about themselves. Embedded in these interactions is the patient's expectation that they must be inevitably abandoned and that any assertion of growth or competence will provoke devastating counterattack that their fragility cannot bear. Caught between their desire to protect themselves from laceration they fear is embedded in the other and, simultaneously, from their need for the other, the therapeutic relationship careens between destructiveness and healing. In part – and I think Shaw has captured something terribly important about another facet of the relationship – such patients are torn between compulsively accommodating the other and counter-phobicly attacking them, as if to show themselves that their own assertion is survivable and that personal expansion is attainable. The rapidly alternating shifts in feeling states that the analyst/therapist must try to read correctly also make therapy with such badly damaged patients both daunting and intimidating. For the patient, such a fractured landscape can contribute to a sense that he or she is crazy, further intensifying their fears and the sense of precariousness they experience.

Quite wonderfully, Shaw points out that even with this group of people, "good enough" work is, indeed, good enough. The therapist who can remain in the embrace of the work that they do with such patients, however imperfectly, can make a meaningful difference, albeit such work, of necessity, must be marked by repeated failures and ruptures that need to be repaired on both sides of the therapeutic fence. In this case, after many years of analytic work, it did indeed seem that Alice was able to tolerate substantial growth in her life, though the therapeutic relationship remained vulnerable to disruption and injury, albeit on a less frequent basis. Shaw also saw (as commented upon in the previous chapter) that for Alice, periods of growth, modest optimism, and personal satisfaction/expansion eventually occasioned regression toward depression and disruptive levels of pain.

I would now like to talk about my own experience working with patients who have been traumatized at the hands of pathological or traumatizing narcissistic others.

As I have commented earlier, I do not feel comfortable citing patient examples, though I readily acknowledge how helpful patient examples are. I will talk about broad groups of dynamics and patient presentations that have seemed to characterize my work in this arena.

Like many practitioners, people that I see who have faced significant narcissistic predation during their childhood and later years have had to bear significant, devastating costs that they struggle to accommodate. Some, I find, have become so damaged that they have effectively given up on themselves, bereft of hope that they can ever feel like a real person or enjoy a sense that they can experience themselves as attractive to others or as welcome in the human community. They movingly express incapacitating despair and pain that they cannot ever imagine transcending. Their sense of self feels so tentative and skeletal, their mistrust and fear of others so unshakable, and their conviction that they are unalterably valueless so deep and so immovable that, even if they remain in therapy for a sustained period of time, they mostly cannot bear to take the risk of growing into the world around them. For those that do take such chances, disappointment and injury that new relationships occasion can decisively defeat them. The therapeutic relationship, to be sure, feels very meaningful and for many such people a virtual lifeline that helps protect them from episodically severe suicidal ideation and/or chronic depression, but many of them seem unable to move beyond their devastating limitations, even though both the patterns that have evolved from them and the origins of their pain are seemingly well understood and even though the empathic bond between therapist and patient appears to be substantial. Some of the people that I have seen who fall into this category are relatively high-functioning individuals (though they would mostly not see themselves that way) while others, of course, are functioning, in the main, in a very erratic and uneven way in the realms of love and work. Seeing such people eventually back away from therapy, sometimes after subjectively heroic efforts, feels tragic. Occasionally such people re-approach me, mounting a more sustained effort that results in substantial success, but many more do not.

People who have been unable to make progress with themselves often eventually talk about their sense that, as they have with others, they anticipate that they must eventually let me down, experiencing themselves unworthy of the effort. To be sure, sustained dedication to the therapeutic work or rededication does expose people to further devastation of hope because the hope that they risk repeatedly fails them. It's hard to share that kind of journey with the people I have just described, but one also has to honor their courage and their wish to advance themselves by being there with them. In the main, I have found the therapeutic relationship is generally not stormy with these people, though it can be episodically or even, on occasion, much more persistently so like the relationship between Daniel Shaw and Alice. One hopes that the therapeutic experience sets the stage for them to try again, perhaps with a different therapist, as they reacquire resilience, but I am also aware that that will not be true for a significant portion of them.

And then there is a significant group of people – perhaps as many as 1/3 of the people I see who've been subjected to severe narcissistic predation – who find the means to create a meaningful identity for themselves that allows them to consummate their uniqueness and express it successfully in the world. Such work is lengthy (several years) and very hard, marked by a very up-and-down course punctuated by severe, episodic despair. Some of this group of people show themselves able to move from a more or less borderline level of functioning toward a cohesive, articulate, well-defined sense of self. In all respects – in both love and work – they can be said to be functioning at a very high level indeed. In spite of such progress, however, like everyone else who suffers the prolonged impact of severe narcissistic invasion during childhood (and perhaps through their adult relationship choices), there

are lingering costs – and not insignificant ones – that they will probably continue to bear throughout the rest of their lives. Their healing, in
other words, is very imperfect but, nonetheless, very substantial. Many
of them will continue to feel intermittently unsafe in the world, particularly at times when they allow their ability to eventuate in success.
Many of them will continue to struggle with hypervigilance and many
of them will find themselves intermittently subject to deep misgivings
about their own value and their place in the world of people. And a
number of them will worry, episodically, about the darkness they are all
too aware that they carry inside, a reflection of all the retaliatory rage
narcissistic predation has generated over the years.

Concerns about voice and the fear of using voice predominate in the
broader patient group. So, too, does shame associated with a sense of
personal emaciation and a conviction that one is unlovable; frightening hunger for relationships and corresponding fear that relationships
can murder one's soul; hunger for success and seemingly intransigent
efforts to sabotage it; exhausting contrivance of self and yearning for
a lasting sense of authenticity; desperation to find peace and a sense
of composure in one's mind versus the reality of tenacious anxiety
disorders that often assume the form of complex PTSD; and tenacious
depressive experience and the wish to find some way to be free of it.
The foregoing, of course, is not a complete list, but perhaps suffices to
capture the nature of the intensity of suffering that such people must
contend with in themselves.

I can identify a limited number of factors that would seem to allow
me to anticipate which of the patients that I see are likely to respond
more successfully to treatment. People who've not been able to push
back against the narcissistic other but instead have confined themselves to a small, crushingly subdued personal space in their effort
to survive seem to find it more challenging to escape the prison that
has "protected" them and find the means to venture into the world of
people. Conversely, patients who have fought back tenaciously against
the narcissistic other, learning to employ many of the same tools of
rage and intimidation the narcissist relies upon to make themselves
feel protected find it very difficult to feel safe enough to relinquish
their combativeness, even though they may be aware of the terrible
costs it imposes on them and the people that they love. To borrow a
very tired concept, people who have forged a "just right" amount of
aggression and accommodation in their attempts to fend off narcissistic predation seemed to do best in treatment. I found that often times

such people had the benefit of a supportive parent who opposed the narcissist and/or supportive others (mentors, coaches, extended family members, friends of the family, etc.) who took a meaningful interest in the person being targeted, either celebrating and affirming their gifts or articulating the pain they were experiencing. And, of course, so-called constitutional givens could make a difference, factors like physical attractiveness, strong empathic gifts, and imposing personal assets (intelligence, proclivity to excel in selected endeavors). Such gifts are often not enough to save some people and, heartbreakingly, merely serve to compound their pain, given the discrepancy between what they recognize they might be versus what they are.

For a more comprehensive discussion of this material, I would refer the reader to Chapter 12, Legacies of Narcissism, in my original book, *A Study of Malignant Narcissism.*

I'd like now, briefly, to recapitulate what I've said about the cornerstone theoretical positions the major theorists we've reviewed have adopted. For Kernberg and his group, grandiose narcissism would appear to be built around a rigid, unyielding sense of grandiosity invested in power and dominance at the expense of constructive interdependence and interrelatedness. Vulnerable narcissism, on the other hand, would seem to be characterized by acute vulnerability (manifest depression and anxiety) and by occult grandiosity that compels people to set punishingly high expectations of themselves that they must meet in order to experience themselves as acceptable to others. In this sense, the Kernberg group would say that their relationships are largely transactional, driven by their need to render themselves acceptable to others and by their need to elicit responses from others that support their self-esteem. The Kernberg group would also say that VN people are drawn to grandiose figures they both envy and need in order to navigate their way through the world.

Both Shaw and Wood, in contrast, distinguish between grandiose and vulnerable narcissism, identifying the former as either traumatizing or pathological narcissism and the latter as a distinct group of people who are struggling with the impact of narcissistic predation who **ought not** to be regarded as narcissistic themselves. Each identifies salient dynamics that they believe characterize these people's personality organization that, for them, meaningfully sets them apart from pathological narcissism. For Wood and probably for Shaw, pathological narcissism in its extreme form includes malignant narcissism. Both Shaw and Wood would largely accept the emphasis that Kernberg places upon grandiosity as the organizing construct around which pathological narcissism is built, but they focus greater attention upon the destructive dynamics that typify narcissistic invasion, including, prominently, subversion of voice and selfhood (so-called soul murder). Wood and Shaw would say that they have limited experience treating pathological or malignant narcissism, finding that both classes of patients are unlikely to seek out treatment for themselves; the majority of their experience derives from working with the class of patients that they see as having been traumatized by NPD's. Kernberg, on the other hand, would say that he and his group have had extensive opportunity to work with NPD and even malignant narcissism in treatment.

In contrast to all four of these theorists, Kohut defines narcissism exclusively as manifestations of grandiosity and idealization in the transference relationship. In his terms, grandiosity and idealization expressed in transference represent attempts to address narcissistic injuries and deficiencies that such patients' life experiences had created for them. As such, these transference manifestations are viewed as, at their core, constructive attempts to heal the self – healing which can maximally take place in an empathic environment that enables the desire to grow. Insight and interpretation in this context are still essential tools, but the therapeutic cast is very different than the aggressive attempts to disrupt grandiosity that would seem to characterize Kernbergian intervention with predominantly GN patients. I have posited that the patients Kernberg and Kohut refer to as narcissistic are, in fact, partially overlapping groups of people; Kernberg appears to be directing attention to both GN and VN, while Kohut largely appears to be preoccupied with understanding what Kernberg would call VN. Indeed, if one examines Kohut's original description of those people he refers to as narcissistic, his description appears to be a very close fit to that group of people the Kernberg group designated as vulnerable narcissists. Parenthetically, it should be noted that Kohut did, albeit briefly, attempt to explore concepts that approximate malignant narcissism (messianic and charismatic narcissism), but, again, his primary interest appeared to be in what Kernberg and others would call the VN group.

References

Shaw, D. (2013). *Traumatic narcissism: Relational systems of subjugation*. Routledge.

Wood, R. (2023). *A study of malignant narcissism: Personal and professional insights*. Routledge.

Chapter 6

Relationship Between Self and Other

In this section of the book, I would like to explore conceptual dimensions that bear upon our understanding of narcissism. As I explore some of the ideas that I will examine in the latter part of the book, I hope to enrich and deepen the reader's grasp of what we mean by the term narcissism. I should clarify that the discussion of narcissistic dimensions that unfolds in the succeeding chapters **largely directs its attention to that form of narcissism which might be considered to be built around the core of a grandiose self – so-called pathological narcissism, Narcissistic Personality Disorder, and malignant narcissism (all forms of predominant GN)**. To include what some clinicians would designate as vulnerable narcissism in the following discussion would unnecessarily reintroduce much of the commentary and analysis that defined the first part of this book.

The first conceptual dimension that I wish to ask my readers to think about is the degree to which people invest in self and in others in narcissistic and in healthy states. In this regard, it may be both instructive and fun to begin with Freud's 1914 paper, "On Narcissism." This paper is seen as a landmark work in which Freud introduced many primary concepts that he elaborated and modified as his work unfolded, including ego libido, object libido, ego ideal, and a related self-observing agency of the psyche that later came to be designated superego. As mentioned in the introduction to this book, Freud was not entirely happy with some of the ideas that he produced, as his friend Ernest Jones (1955, p. 340) tells us. This paper did not represent the first time that Freud and others had discussed narcissism. The editor of "On Narcissism," James Strachey, reported that "a paper on the subject by Rank, mentioned by Freud at the beginning of the present study,

DOI: 10.4324/9781032649535-6

was published in 1911, and other references by Freud himself soon followed: e. g. in section III of the Schreiber analysis (1911c) and in Totem and Taboo (1912–13), Standard Ed., **13**, 88–90" (editor's note from the Standard Edition, pp. 69–70).

As one reads the 1914 paper, one can indeed feel Freud struggling to articulate the dynamic forces that he imagined might define narcissism. The foundation of these dynamics derived largely from his attempts to appreciate libidinal forces that he believed helped govern the psyche. By libidinal, he appeared to mean sources of psychic energy that were either sexual, self-preservational, or interpersonal in nature. At least some of the difficulty that he encountered in his exposition arose because he conceived of these libidinous forces as being part of a largely closed hydraulic system in which energy gained by one part of the psyche imposed loss in another. Self-preservational energy (ego libido) helped the ego fuel its efforts to survive, while interpersonal energy (object libido) supported engagement with other people. In identifying both self-preservational libido and interpersonal libido Freud was acknowledging for the first time that there were, indeed, nonsexual sources of energy that the human psyche could draw upon to carry out its essential operations.

Freud went on to explain that energy the psyche invested in its relationships with other people could be considered to derive from self-preservational energy or ego libido:

> Thus we form the idea of there being an original libidinal cathexis of the ego, from which some is later given off to the objects, but which fundamentally persists and is related to the object cathexis much as the body of an amoeba is related to the pseudopodia which it puts out. (p. 75)

In this framework, there was "an antithesis between ego libido and object libido. The more of the one is employed, the more the other becomes depleted" (p. 76).

In elaborating upon this antithesis, Freud noted that "the individual actually does carry on a twofold existence: one to serve his own purposes and the other as a link in a chain, which he serves against his will, or at least involuntarily" (p. 78). In this passage, he seems to be referring to the involuntary urge to spread seed, but he also adds that "the separation of the sexual instincts from the ego instincts would simply reflect this twofold function of the individual" (p. 78). Does Freud mean to imply that our engagement with other people is irresistible, therefore compelling us to act as a link in the social chain? I don't think it's clear. What he does want us to understand is that the energy we invest in our relationships can also be withdrawn from them (his pseudopodia analogy), creating a secondary form of narcissism as the individual turns away from the world of people. In extreme form, such withdrawal may produce a retreat into a psychotic world that may prove to be impervious to external influence.

Later in his 1914 paper, Freud reframes his understanding of the relationship between sexual and ego libido, telling us that, because "the auto-erotic sexual satisfactions are experienced in connection with vital functions which serve the purpose of self-preservation," (p. 87) sexual libido or pleasure can be seen to emerge as a consequence of ego libido. In other words, inasmuch as our instinct for self-preservation exposes us to the pleasure we experience when we address self-preservational needs, we awaken the sexual energy that comes to play such a vital part in our lives. In this formulation (there were to be many later re-formulations), sexual energy, which he had deemed to be primary and foundational to his theoretical conception of the psyche, now seemingly moves into a secondary position.

But if there is secondary narcissism, what does Freud mean by primary narcissism? Freud tells us that "we say that a human being has originally two sexual objects – himself and the woman who nurses him – and in so doing we are postulating a primary narcissism in everyone, which may in some cases manifest itself in a dominating fashion in his object choice" (p. 88).

In a preceding paragraph, Freud conveys what he means by "in a dominating fashion," alerting us that "… in people whose libidinal development has suffered some disturbance, such as perverts and homosexuals, that in their later choice of love objects they have taken as a model not their mother but their own selves. They are plainly seeking *themselves* as a love object and are exhibiting a type of object choice which must be termed 'narcissistic.' In this observation we have the strongest of reasons which have led us to adopt the hypothesis of narcissism" (p. 88).

Choosing one's self as the object of one's own love was considered a narcissistic choice and choosing someone else to love whose attraction derived from early caregiving relationships was recognized as an anaclitic choice.

While the simplicity of Freud's conception of primary narcissism can at least be said to be characterized by a measure of internal coherence, it does not of course capture contemporary attitudes toward sexuality. The distinction that Freud draws between primary and secondary narcissism, however, is one that clinicians have struggled with throughout their attempts to understand narcissism over a course of many decades. Before taking up this subject at greater length, however, I want to draw us back into further exploration of the topic at hand: investment in self-versus investment in others.

Freud's appreciation of the energy dynamic that defined the human psyche led him to conclude that "complete object love of the attachment type is, properly speaking, characteristic of the male" (p. 88). Complete object love would seem to fall within the realm of anaclitic choice. Freud went on to explain:

> Women, especially if they grow up with good looks, develop a certain self contentment which compensates them for the social restrictions that are imposed upon them in their choice of object. Strictly speaking, it is only themselves such women love with an intensity comparable to that of the man's love for them. Nor does their need lie in the direction of loving, but of being loved; and the man who fulfills this condition is the one finds favor with them. The importance of this type of woman for the erotic life of mankind is to be rated very high. (p. 89)

He also allowed that even for this narcissistically oriented group of women, there was a pathway to "complete object love" – through maternal love – but the caveat was that women could enjoy such fulfillment largely because the child that they bore was a product of their own body (i.e., as a narcissistic extension of themselves, that is to say, as a derivative of self-love, which therefore facilitated deeper investment).

Freud did consider that there were, in fact, "quite a number" of women who were capable of loving in the way that men did (who did so according to "the masculine type"), over investing in the people that they cared about as they were drawn into a loving relationship (p. 89). Women who are more like men, in other words, were conceived as possessing greater capacity to love.

Probably in response to the potentially unsettling implications of his remarks, Freud assured his readers that his characterization of women was "not due to any tendentious desire on my part to depreciate women" (p. 89).

In actuality, male capacity to love and even parental love was deeply tainted by narcissistic self-interest in the Freudian framework. In part, Freud argued in 1914, men fell in love because they tended to choose women who approximated parts of their ego ideal or imagined ideal self, reflecting back that which they most admired in themselves or even that which was deficient in the self. Much the same could be said for parents who saw themselves in their child, gushing about the child's attractiveness even though any objective observer could see that such praise was not deserved.

"Parental love, which is so moving and at bottom so childish, is nothing but the parents' narcissism born-again, which, transformed into object love, unmistakably reveals its former nature" (p. 91).

One hears in this formulation what one hesitates to call a deep cynicism about humankind's ability to exceed its own narcissistic interests and truly love/embrace another's uniqueness. Freud is giving us a foretaste of an important theme in narcissism literature: that our compulsion to invest – and often overinvest – in the self stands in the way of our potential to express deep, genuine loving feelings for others.

From a Freudian perspective, love, then, was a transactional undertaking in which one traded narcissistic supplies between the self and the other.

In his 1914 paper, he also offers us a vision of what true happiness is: "to be their own ideal once more, in regard to sexual no less than other trends, as they were in childhood – that is what people strive to attain as their happiness" (p. 100). As he did earlier in his paper, Freud imagines that the unlimited adoration and celebration that attends early life – a state he refers to as "his Majesty the baby" – provides us with a taste of ecstasy that we seek to replicate throughout our lives by pursuing the narcissistic bliss babyhood occasioned. This was a pull that had to be resisted if one was to transcend the struggle with the reality principle so that we might learn to endure and perhaps even exceed the normal miseries of everyday life.

Striking disagreements began to emerge about the concept of primary narcissism. Balint (1960), for instance, believed the infant was fused harmoniously with his environment in a state he called primary love. Any narcissism that emerged in the infant's life could be seen to be a consequence of frustrations and disruptions that the environment visited upon him. All narcissism, in this conception, would be considered to be secondary narcissism. Primary narcissism did not exist for Balint.

Melanie Klein, in contrast, conceived of a savage early environment in which the infant was buffeted between the ministrations of a good mother (the good breast) and the subjectively experienced neglect of a bad mother (the bad breast). The relentless promptings of the infant's pressing needs for comfort and satiety imbued his world with frightening, roller coaster uncertainties that moved him back and forth between pleasure and emotions like rage and fear. In response to a brutal, shearing environment that sometimes gave and sometimes withheld, the infant constructed internal representations of his experiences that split his world and the people in it into pieces marked by polarized good and bad imagery. This first, very divided representational world of the child Klein designated as the paranoid-schizoid position. His Majesty the baby enjoyed very little stability in Klein's appreciation of the infant's reality. It was only by degree that the child could begin to escape this nightmarish existence as he started to recognize that the same mother who fed him was the same mother who disappointed him. As the child learned to integrate both mothers into a single whole – a mother who was sometimes responsive and sometimes not – he could begin to move past his early distortions and accept the imperfections his world presented him. Obviously, the mother's capacity to help the child reinterpret his world and acquire the means to soothe himself was critical. This stage – a reality-based fusion of both the fulfilling and frustrating aspects of relationships – was termed the depressive stage. Once the depressive stage had been actualized, people became capable of holding contradictory ideas in place at the same time, were better equipped to engage in nuanced thinking, and could better tolerate ambiguity.

Klein believed that these early experiences – the shifts between the paranoid schizoid position and the depressive one – constituted vulnerabilities that could reassert themselves in later life when an individual was confronted with powerful threat that impelled him to abandon the nuanced thinking of an adult depressive position for a more archaic bipolar world. The ease with which the paranoid-schizoid position could reassert itself was thought to be a reflection of the degree of resilience his relations with other people had imparted to him.

Jacobson (1964) took the position that a newly born child could not differentiate his own sensations from the people (objects) whose interaction with him produced them. He described this early state of being as a state of undifferentiated symbiotic fusion rather than primary narcissism or primary love. To Jacobson's mind, only as the infant began to distinguish the difference between himself and others could concepts like primary and secondary narcissism become meaningful. In this framework, perhaps in some ways like Kohut, the newly articulated representation of self could be expected to be fragile, vulnerable, and lacking in cohesion.

I described these three examples, which are but three among many, so that the reader can appreciate that there was not clear consensus about the realities that defined the infant's subjectivity, never mind anything like clear agreement about a conceptual entity like primary narcissism. Consider some of the comments that relatively more contemporary theorists have offered about the subject following intense exploration of this topic.

Meissner (2008) reflected that: "this basic concept of primary narcissism has undergirded all subsequent analytic thinking about narcissism ... If one can consider such an objectless state, it can at best have only limited application... It would be rapidly eroded as the neonate becomes increasingly object related and object responsive.... The concept of primary narcissism is fraught with difficulties, not the least being whether any such entity or process ever exists. There is no evidence to demonstrate it, only its postulation as a component of the instinctual drive theory..." (pp. 464–465). Meissner then adds that drive theory's "entire system of hydraulics is suspect and has in large measure been found wanting and does not measure up to the standards of scientific acceptability. The inherent ambiguities and internal contradictions of the concept of primary narcissism and the outmoded model of psychic organization and developmental progression it implies led me to conclude that analytic theorizing about the self would be far better off without the concept of primary narcissism" (p. 466). Importantly, Meissner emphasizes that "we have no way of knowing what the quality of mental processes in the infant brain might be, so that attributions of narcissistic forms of thought or self-appraisal are based on no more than pure conjecture and even adultomorphic projection" (p. 467).

In a similar manner, Hinze (2017) asserted that "we can discard Freud's speculations (1914) about auto eroticism and primary narcissism because we know nowadays that these phases do not exist"

(p. 24). Like Meissner, she commented that "There is a specific difficulty among psychoanalysts to get rid of outworn concepts that are
no longer useful" (p. 24).

Hinze also commented upon our hunger for joyful states of fusion:

> this phase (referring to early infancy) is not a paradise like merger
> with Mother without experiencing any tension. Later in life we
> can indulge in fantasies of fusion, of being one with some primary
> object. But these states of mind are not returns to a really lived
> through paradise. They are based on a fantasy of a wished-for state
> of primary narcissism we never really lived through. (p. 31)

For Hinze, as they were for Klein, object relations were primary.
The child's developmental course was built around dealing with others
and "idealizing and internalizing may be the means to cope with the
otherness of the object" (p. 31).

This quote now brings us back to the focus of this section, the degree of investment in self and others that characterizes narcissistic and
healthy states of being.

Let us now re-consider the idea that energy spent in one part of the
psyche is lost to the other. Within the context of relatively healthy psychological functioning, clinicians like Kernberg (1975) recognized that:

> Normally, an increase of libidinal investment of the self also re-
> sults in an increase in the libidinal investment in objects: a self
> with increased libidinal investment, at peace and happy with itself,
> so to speak, is able to invest more in external objects and their in-
> ternalized representations. In general, when there is an increase of
> narcissistic investment, there is a parallel increase in the capacity
> to love and to give… Metaphorically speaking, the charging of the
> battery of the self induces secondarily a recharging of the battery of
> libidinal investment in objects. (pp. 320–321)

The more reality-based self-esteem that one enjoys, the more love
one has to give and the easier it is to care about people. Though not
quite said directly, one hears in Kernberg's words the strong intimation
that the act of loving another – in addition to the love and the esteem
that one has for oneself – is in some ways deeply pleasurable, generating energy all on its own.

In contrast, Kealy and Ogrodniczuk (2014) tell us that "pathological narcissism is a form of maladaptive self-regulation that impedes the capacity to love. Although narcissism is often construed as excessive self-love, individuals with pathological narcissism are impaired in being able to love themselves as well as others" (p. 101).

They assess "the capacity to give and receive love (as) arguably the most valuable acquisition available," adding that "those who struggle to love and to feel love may be acutely aware of painful feelings associated with their plight, while others may attempt to hide or override their difficulties" (p. 101).

In the first section of the book, we have already discussed, at length, many of the obstacles that an investment in a narcissist position creates for us as we attempt to love others and even ourselves. As a means of briefly recapitulating some of those ideas, I would again refer the reader to Kealy and Ogrodniczuk's cogent summary of Kernberg's views about this subject. They remind us (as noted earlier in this book) that Kernberg believed pathological narcissism represented an investment in a distorted version of the self absent its failings, shortfalls, vulnerabilities, and needs rather than an overinvestment. To which one can add, how indeed could one also love others in the context of such profound psychic distortions?

Ferruta and Carmody beautifully capture the paradox that is pathological narcissism – which they define as an attempt to create an illusion that the narcissist is able to do without the other.

Within a psychoanalytic framework, our relationships with other people are deemed to be foundational to our efforts to create personhood for ourselves. And this assumption seems to dominate the clinical world whether one believes that a rudimentary self exists from birth onward or only emerges through one's interactions with others (see Hinze, 2017, for a list of theoreticians who fall on one side of this fence or the other). She posited that "nowadays most analysts assume a certain degree of object relatedness from birth on" (p. 27). Mollon (1986), as commented upon earlier, drew attention to Kohut's belief that an infant was both separate and partially merged with others, reflecting two separate lines of narcissistic development (merger with self-objects) and object love (relatedness to separate objects). These two lines of development could be conceived as self-esteem (love for the self) and love for others.

Clarke (2011), writing, references Kohon's appreciation of Fairbairn's work:

> The instincts are not pleasure seeking but object seeking;... Since there are object relations from beginning of life, this presupposes the existence of an early ego, or self.
>
> (Kohon, 1986, p. 22)

In the context of this discussion, it is irresistible, of course, not to mention Melanie Klein's famous quote about the importance of object relations that emerged in the context of her work with young children:

> That there is no instinctual urge, no anxiety situation, no mental process which does not involve objects, external or internal... Furthermore, love and hatred, fantasies, anxieties and defenses are also operative from the beginning and are indivisibly linked with object relations.
>
> (Klein, 1952)

There appears to be consensus – not surprisingly – that psychic growth, whether it evolves in a pathological or healthy direction, is inextricably bound up in our relationships with other people from the very beginning of life. Now let's see, in a very broad stroke way, what kind of core challenges our relationships with other people generate for us – challenges that are particularly pertinent to the evolution of either healthy or pathological narcissism.

Blatt (2008) has drawn an important and very useful distinction between needs for self-definition (which he refers to as introjective needs) and our need for other people (anaclitic needs). Somewhat similarly, Bernardi and Eidlin (2018) suggest that "a dialectical balance between the recognition that comes from oneself and the recognition that comes from others" is necessary for any given personality to establish for him or herself (p. 307). Similarly, Cartwright (2016) describes an opposition between egocentric tendencies and socio-centric tendencies. Fossati et al. (2015) defined anaclitic psychopathology as an attempt to sustain relationships with others at the expense of identity and introjective psychopathology as an attempt to maintain identity at the expense of one's relationships. They additionally argued that focus upon these two axes was compatible with our evolving appreciation of attachment theory. Gabbard (1993) nicely captured the tension inherent in the pull between the desire to merge with a lover versus the need to maintain separateness and selfhood. The greater the hunger for merger, the more one is likely to experience anxiety about the dissolution of self. To protect the self, hatred about minor differences is mobilized and inflated to distance the other.

Ferruta and Carmody (2012) very effectively describe the essence of negotiation between self and others that must take place in both the interpersonal and intrapsychic world:

> While the subject aspires to oneness with the object, it is however true that this re-unifying obliges the ego to modify its organization, with the risk of being invaded and replaced by the object, or to go into freefall when faced with the object being too far removed from it or definitively taking its leave. (p. 22)

They cite a poignant passage from Giuseppe Di Chiara (1985), who comments that "therefore the main function of the ego in mental development is to make room for the other inside oneself: room to welcome him, without mixing oneself up with him" (pp. 459–460).

Bollas (1992), who is also quoted by Ferruta and Carmody, further elaborates on the interpersonal challenge we all face when we enter into relationships with others:

> To be a character is to enjoy the risk of being processed by the object – indeed, to seek objects, in part, in order to be metamorphosed, as one "goes through" change by going through the processional moment provided by any object's integrity. Each entry into an experience of an object is rather like being born again, as subjectivity is newly informed by the encounter, its history altered by a radically effective present that will change its structure. (p. 59)

Ferutta and Carmody remind us that "… we are continually created and re-created by encounters with the world of objects which allows us to be what we did not know we could become" (p. 30).

The psychic intimacy of our everyday exchanges with one another is quite astonishing; they would seem to presuppose an intact, relatively coherent sense of self many of us would not feel we possess that can tolerate the impact of the other on one's own psychological landscape – indeed, not only tolerate it but, frequently, welcome it, experiencing the interchange and the resulting transformation of self as a source of joy or inspiration or comfort or even self-correction. For me, this conceptualization does very accurately capture what it feels like to have a relationship with someone else. This conceptualization also implies that most of us will have the resilience (even though we may not feel like we do) to endure the bruising and the violation that is sometimes part of our social interchanges. It means that somewhere inside we believe we can either repair or mitigate ruptures in ourselves, in our relationships, and/or in our friends and survive the process if an attachment fails, somehow possessing more or less enough hope about ourselves to imagine that, in spite of the pain we may have to endure, we can probably move on and create better realities for ourselves. This is, obviously, often quite a terrifying process for many of us, one that has the potential to create significant or even catastrophic personal disruption, particularly if our sense of self is fragile. But our need for relationships is so profoundly felt, in spite of the enduring pain they may occasion for us, that we pursue them, feeling, as both Fairbairn (1952) and Ogden (1986) have suggested, that it is better to have a bad relationship than no relationship.

Even at the very best of times and in the presence of considerable support, significant disruptions in our relationships can be profoundly compromising. But it is these very human transactions – our connections – that sustain us so that most of us will need to come back and seek out relationships in some form in spite of the risk. Without them, we really do lose ourselves, our place in the world, and the means through which we provide ourselves with the psychic sustenance (love and friendship) that we need to either endure or even to flourish in some fashion. Pathologically narcissistic personalities, however, can separate themselves away from the casual social intercourse that is so necessary for the rest of us, attempting to insulate themselves from any impact the other can have upon them. The result, as we saw in the first section of the book, is a personality that protects itself with rage, contempt, and perpetual combat, invading and dominating the other before they themselves can be invaded. The consequence of adopting this defense is, as we observed, a solipsistic existence, a blighted interior, ofttimes consignment to a paranoid world, and an inability to establish deep, meaningful attachments with others. In these terms, narcissistic disorders can be construed to be introjective ones, reflecting disproportionate concern about identity and the need to inure oneself against healthy interpenetration with other personalities.

Judith Teicholz (1978) observed that Freud's definition of narcissism as a libidinal investment in the self (the implication being overinvestment) was still the predominant view, in spite of various theoretical advances that had unfolded in our conceptualization of the psyche. Writing just two years later, Kingston (1980) suggested that there were two broad trends in clinicians' thinking about narcissism – first, a view of narcissism as a defensive retreat from object relations and second, a grasp of narcissism as a reflection of a particular kind of relationship that one establishes with the self. To these definitions, we might also add Shaw's view of narcissism as a particular kind of relational system that the narcissist establishes with himself and the world around him.

Before completing the discussion of investment in self versus others, it is probably timely to reflect upon the concept of self, which has been a source of contention in psychoanalytic literature, as the discussion that unfolds below will briefly illustrate.

Smith (1985) tells us that Freud used the term ego "in four distinct senses: as a representation of oneself, as the executive apparatus of the personality, as the inferred source of choice and volition, and as the origin of the sense of identity (… ego feeling)" (p. 494). He concluded that Freud probably believed he was describing four facets of what he thought of as a unitary phenomenon, confusingly moving back and forth between different meanings of ego in a single paragraph. Smith felt Federn was the first analyst to underscore a subjective sense of personal identity as an ego phenomenon, alternating between this appreciation of ego and a sense that ego was some kind of apparatus, which Smith judged was imprecise. Teicholz (1978) felt that it was inevitable that the study of the self would emerge as a focal point in analytic literature, given its focus upon object relations (i.e., the relationship between others and oneself). Even as late as 1978, she reflected that there was still uncertainty about what self was: it had been "viewed primarily as a substructure within the ego (Hartmann and Loewenstein, 1962); as an outcome of structure (Modell, 1968); and… primarily in experiential and phenomenological terms (Lichtenberg, 1975; Klass and Offenkrantz, 1976)" (p. 832). Kohut, of course, placed an evolving sense of self at the very center of psychic development, creating an eponymous school of analytic thought. For him, as we have already considered, emerging sense of self was the very glue that both defined and held a personality together, contingent upon the quality of interaction the self enjoyed with the people around it. For Kernberg, self could only be differentiated in response to interaction with other people, interaction that enabled differentiation between others and the emerging self. Beres (1981) took the position that the construct "self" added very little to our understanding of the human experience and the insights that structural theory, ego psychology, and drive theory provided. He complained that Kohut's conception of self-created an entity out of abstraction, surprisingly asserting that patients were not aware of something called self nor were they in a position to be able to either understand or know what self was.

Pulver (1970) asked us to consider that differing ego states comprise the self and each was possessed of its own distinctive affective links, introducing further complexity into our attempts to appreciate what self was. Hartmann and Loewenstein (1962) prompted us to consider that self was, in effect, a kind of moving target, dependent upon "later objects the person takes as his models and the value systems of his cultural environment..." (p. 76).

For me, Meissner (2008) provides a helpful way of dealing with the conundrum of self:

> I would suggest that the important parameters of psychological development have to do with the separation, organization, and individuation of an authentic sense of self. In more specifically structural terms, this process can be addressed from the standpoint of the differentiation and integration of the self system, or self organization, in relation to the emerging organization of functional capacities as aspects of self functioning. The self system... is related to and affected by the developmental course of other aspects of psychic integration, including motivational patterns, object relations, ego functions and capacities, superego integration, forms of internalization, etc.... (There are) diverse and complex factors contributing to the development of the self that have little or nothing to do with narcissism. (p. 472)

Meissner goes on to explain, however, that "the self requires a fundament of narcissistic motivations both for normal development and for normal functioning (citing Grunberger, 1971/1979). Narcissism embraces the spectrum of motivational states serving as normal complements of mature functioning. Narcissism provides the self-sustaining and enhancing moments of comfort, gratification, self-regard, self-confidence, peace of mind, inner tranquility, self-respect, balance, in addition to those specified by Kohut (1966) as mature transformations of narcissism – creativity, empathy, the capacity to contemplate one's own impermanence and death, sense of humor, and wisdom" (p. 476).

Consistent with Meissner's framework, however, narcissistic disorder was considered to be a consequence of the confluence of forces – both developmental and narcissistic – that shaped a given individual. Like other clinicians who conceived of narcissism as a retreat from object relatedness, Meissner concluded that "where narcissism begins to substitute, by way of fantasy or otherwise, for investment in real objects or the capacity for investment in objects, the result begins to look pathological" (p. 479). He is also asking us to recognize, however, that narcissistic disorders grow primarily out of structural faults in the self – very much like Kohut – rather than being a consequence of a narcissistic cathexis of the self, but his "self" – unlike Kohut – is instead a complex self-system subject to multiplicities of forces besides narcissistic investments. Meissner's self-system provides us with a framework that allows us to embrace the rich findings that developmental psychology and attachment theory have to offer us, permitting us to integrate them into psychoanalytic thought.

Meissner has offered us, in my estimate, a much more differentiated, albeit more complex, view of the interrelationship of self, of narcissism, and of maturational processes that give us the means to further extend our understanding of all three constructs.

In the context of the discussion that has just unfolded about self and about narcissistic functions, please bear in mind that there are many other clinicians possessed of many other points of view who have not been represented in the narrative I have provided. Concerns about space had to predominate. My hope is that the reader now has an even fuller appreciation of the complexities that attend our grasp of self and its relationship to narcissism.

Our exposition of the relationship between investment in self and object side-by-side, an enhanced appreciation of what self means, lays the groundwork for a better understanding of the difference between healthy versus pathological narcissism. Consider the following appraisals.

Stolorow (1975) maintained that a stable, successful internalized sense of value that can be sustained independently of the influence of others can be seen to be reflective of a successful narcissistic adjustment; in contrast, dependence upon an idealized other to maintain identity and personal value would represent a less satisfactory narcissistic equilibrium. Bernardi and Eidlin (2018) believed that whether there was a preponderance of VN or GN in a given personality, so long as there was also a constructive balance between the needs to appreciate oneself and to be appreciated by others, an individual likely possessed the means and the resilience to accommodate many of the narcissistic injuries that life might create. Meissner (2008), as we have seen, placed emphasis upon the importance of establishing ego boundaries and stability if healthy narcissism was to be protected. He further commented that "good healthy narcissism as a form of self-esteem (was) based on pleasurable self-images and bad narcissism in the form of excessively high self-regard (was) based on defense against underlying unpleasurable images" (p. 481). Teicholz (1968) cites Schafer's (1968) grasp of healthy and pathological narcissism. Healthy narcissism was seen to depend primarily on positive self and object representations growing out of early childhood experience, the maintenance and regulation of which could thus be guaranteed with a minimum of defensive efforts and conflict and a maximal degree of "neutrality, stability, and nourishing satisfaction" (Schafer, 1968, p. 192). Alternatively, pathological narcissism could be conceived of as consisting of primarily negative self and object representations which led to a preponderance of psychic energy being directed towards self-protective ends and/or toward "the devious means (an individual) uses to secure satisfactions and revenge" (Schafer, 1968, p. 192).

For Bolognini and Garfield (2008) healthy narcissism was framed as necessary narcissism, i.e., as the amount of narcissism required to ensure the self felt acceptable and lovable to others. They identified a number of factors that they relied upon to help define necessary narcissism, including a willingness to invest the self in other people, capacity to distinguish the self from others, cohesiveness of the self, realistic appraisal of one's own limitations and proportions, and confirmation of a stable internal self-representation. Auerbach (1990), citing fascinating social psychology research (Taylor and Brown, 1988; Emmons, 1987), provides us with a sense of what necessary narcissism might look like: not an accurate appraisal of self-esteem but one that provides an overly positive view of the self side-by-side exaggerated perception of one's sense of control, mastery, and optimism.

Hinze (2017) asserts that there is no self without an object and no object without a self. As such, the self that cannot recognize the authenticity or the existence of the other cannot love. Pulver (1970) argued that narcissism could be conceived of as either a lack of object relationships or as a state in which the self's subjective realities played a more vital role than the actualities that the object embodied. Auerbach (1990) recapitulated Bach's work, reflecting that, in Bach's framework, the narcissistic self is experienced as cohesive and vital at the cost of objects becoming fragmented and lifeless, and vice versa. Smith (1988) noted that both Federn and Kohut believed that the antithesis to narcissism was not object relations but object love.

One hears in many of these definitional appraisals of narcissistic health and pathology an unmistakable emphasis upon the importance of object relations or, more simply put, our relationships with other people. If one was exposed to caring, kind, loving, compassionate others who provided a more or less accurate appraisal of one's internal realities in the formative years, one was likely to be possessed of a reservoir of rewarding relational representations that, in turn, could be expected to create a strong sense of personal value and a healthy fund of personal resilience. In the absence of sustaining experiences with other people and in the context of damaging or wounding relationships, one was left with a repository of distressing imagery that turned one away from other people and that compelled one to engage in a variety of self and other destructive defenses, all reflective of narcissistic injury. Also implicit in many of the comments that have just been reviewed was the sense that health was demarcated by an individual's ability to stand apart from others and express an authentic self even though doing so might expose him or her to others' disapproval. Such an individual would be someone, in Hannah Arendt's terms, who could think, feel, and act even though a malevolent surround might try to impose destructive choices on them. Moreover, it could be seen that such an individual's realities would be informed not only by self-love, but by a corresponding capacity to love and value others. Their willingness to celebrate their uniqueness in the context of their relationships with others would also help mitigate concern about identity, which, as we have seen, is an inherent part of coming together with someone else.

At the other end of the spectrum the pathological and/or malignant narcissist would also show themselves capable of standing apart from others and of standing by their voice, but with important differences. Their posture, as we have noted, would be marked by profound self-interest, a lack of empathy, an investment in destroying others' subjectivities, and rigid, unyielding adherence to the prerogatives of power and dominance.

Meissner reminds us that in addition to its pathological forms, it is also important for us to recognize narcissism as "a natural resource, rooted in basic inclinations which can be diverted to serve and support man's best interest" (p. 477).

References

Auerbach, J. (1990). Narcissism. *Psychoanalytic Psychology, 7*(4), 545–564.

Balint, M. (1960). Primary narcissism and primary love. *The Psychoanalytic Quarterly, 29*(1), 6–43.

Bernardi, R., & Eidlin, M. (2018). Thin-skinned or vulnerable narcissism and thick-skinned or grandiose narcissism: similarities and differences. *International Journal of Psychoanalysis, 99*(2), 291–313.

Beres, D. (1981). Self, identity, and narcissism. *Psychoanalytic Quarterly, 50*, 515–534.

Blatt, S. J. (2008). *Polarities of experience: Relatedness and self-definition in personality, development, psychopathology, and the therapeutic process.* American Psychological Association.

Bollas, C. (1992). *Being a character.* Routledge.

Bolognini, S., & Garfield, M. (2008). Reconsidering narcissism from a contemporary, complex psychoanalytic view. *International Forum of Psychoanalysis, 17*(2), 104–111.

Cartwright, D. (2016). A bionic formulation of shame: The terror of becoming oneself. *International Journal of Psychoanalysis Open, 3*, 68.

Clarke, G. (2011). On: The narcissism of minor differences. *International Journal of Psychoanalysis, 92*(1), 231–233.

Di Chiara, G. (1985). Una Prospettive Psicoanalitica del dopo Freud: Un posto per l'altro. *Rivista di Psicoanalisi, 31*(4), 451–461.

Fairbairn, W. R. D. (1952). *Psychoanalytic studies of the personality.* Routledge.

Ferruta, A., & Carmody, C. (2012). Continuity or discontinuity between healthy and pathological narcissism. *Italian Psychoanalytic Annual, 6*, 19–33.

Fossati, A., Feeney, J., Pincus, A., Borroni, S., & Maffei, C. (2015). The structure of pathological narcissism and its relationships with adult attachment styles. *Psychoanalytic Psychology, 32*(3), 403–431.

Freud, S. (1914). On narcissism. *Standard Edition, 14*, 67–102.

Gabbard, G. (1993). On hate in love relationships: The narcissism of minor differences revisited. *The Psychoanalytic Quarterly, 62*, 229–238.

Grunberger, B. (1979). *Narcissism: Psychoanalytic essays.* International Universities Press (original work published in 1971).

Hartmann, H., & Loewenstein, R. (1962). Notes on the superego. In *Papers on psychoanalytic psychology* (Psychol. Issues, Monogr. 14). International Universities Press.

Hinze, E. (2017). Narcissism: Is it still a useful psychoanalytic concept? *Romanian Journal of Psychoanalysis*, *10*(2), 19–34.

Jacobson, E. (1964). *The self and the object world.* International Universities Press.

Jones, E. (1955). *The life and work of Sigmund Freud. Vol. II Years of Maturity, 1901–1919* (pp. 340). Hogarth Press.

Kealy, D., & Ogrudniczuk, J. (2014). Pathological narcisisism and the obstruction of love. *Psychodynamic Psychiatry*, *42*(1), 101–119.

Kernberg, O. F. (1975). *Borderline conditions and pathological narcissism.* Jason Aronson.

Kohut, H. (1966). Forms and transformations of narcissism. *Journal of the American Psychoanalytic Association*, *14*, 243–272.

Kingston, W. (1980). A theoretical and technical approach to narcissistic disturbance. *International Journal of Psychoanalysis*, *61*, 383–394.

Klass, D., & Offenkrantz, W. (1976). Sartre's contribution to the understanding of narcissism. *International Journal of Psychoanalysis*, *5*, 547–565.

Klein, M. (1952). The origins of transference. *International Journal of Psychoanalysis*, *33*, 433–438.

Kohon, G. (1986). *The British school of psychoanalysis: The independent tradition.* Free Association Books.

Lichtenberg, J. D. (1975). The development of the sense of self. *American Psychoanalytic Association*, *23*, 453–484.

Meissner, S. J. (2008). Narcissism and the self: Psychoanalytic considerations. *The Journal of the American Academy of Psychoanalysis and Dynamic Psychiatry*, *36*(3), 461–494.

Modell, A. H. (1968). *Object love and reality.* International Universities Press.

Mollon, P. (1986). An appraisal of Kohut's contribution to the understanding of narcissism. *British Journal of Psychotherapy*, *3*(2), 151–161.

Ogden, T. H. (1986). *The matrix of the mind: Object relations and the psychoanalytic dialogue.* Aronson.

Pulver, S. E. (1970). Narcissism: The term and concept. *Journal of the American Psychoanalytic Association*, *18*, 319–341.

Schafer, R. (1968). *Aspects of internalization.* International Universities Press.

Smith, D. (1985). Freud's developmental approach to narcissism: A concise review. *The International Journal of Psychoanalysis*, *66*, 489–497.

Smith, D. (1988). Narcissism since Freud: Towards a unified theory. *British Journal of Psychotherapy*, *4*(3), 302–312.

Stolorow, R. (1975). Towards a functional definition of narcissism. *International Journal of Psychoanalysis*, *56*, 179–185.

Taylor, S. E., & Brown, J. D. (1988). Illusion and well-being: A social psychological perspective on mental health. *Psychological Bulletin*, *103*, 193–210.

Teicholz, J. (1978). A selective review of psychoanalytic literature on theoretical conceptualizations of narcissism. *Journal of the American Psychoanalytic Association*, *26*, 831–861.

Chapter 7

Narcissism as a Defense
Brief Consideration of Etiology

A theme that has wound its way in and out of our discussion is the con-ceptualization of narcissism as a defense meant to protect the psyche from unbearable and catastrophic outcomes. Particular attention will focus upon the role that envy and a sense of personal cohesion play in narcissistic dynamics in the narrative that follows.

Stolorow (1975) details Kernberg's (1970) appreciation of narcis-sism as a "defensive retreat from dreaded object relationships charac-terized by intense dependency, oral envy and primitive oral sadism, and the resulting guilt and fears of retaliation" (p. 180). Elder (1986) draws attention to Hannah Segal's interpretation of Melanie Klein's paper, "envy and gratitude" (1957), in which the latter identifies projective identification as a means through which the projector can get inside the other person and takeover/displace their qualities, thereby offsetting the distress which envy causes. Segal was said to believe that Klein's comments were suggestive of an intimate relationship between narcis-sism and envy. Segal reminds us that, within a Kleinian framework, the discovery of the separateness of an object evokes intense envy that goodness and vitality lie outside the self. Elder also focused her reader's attention upon Rosenfeld's (1971) work. Rosenfeld posited that the fusion between self and other, which characterized narcissistic states, could be conceptualized as a defense against having to recog-nize the separateness of the object. Rosenfeld also pointed out that envy was likely to grow out of dependence and the implicit recognition that it occasioned of the other's goodness. Spillius (1983) considered that the denial of dependence, which was central to a narcissistic pos-ture, served the aim of denying both envy and need. Seidler (1999), in-terestingly, related envy to "'wishing to belong.' The fulfillment of this

DOI: 10.4324/9781032649535-7

desire appears unobtainable. Destroying the original aim of the desire is then a way of eliminating the pain of being excluded" (p. 295). Gabbard (1993) also identified envy as a prominent force that underlies the mobilization of hatred that he believed protected identity in the face of impulsion to merge with a loved other.

Let's now explore what we mean by envy in more depth.

It is Berke (whom we visited earlier), however, who seemingly best articulated the dynamics of envy in his 1985 paper, "Envy loveth not: A study of the origin, influence and confluence of envy and narcissism." Berke boldly states that "envy is an inborn, destructive, motivating force, opposed to love and antagonistic to life" (p. 171). He noted that Freud (1915, p. 139) described this passion as a hatred "older than love." Berke felt Freud's description "fit a rudimentary envy, which averts love and transforms intense interest and excited desire into malevolence" (p. 171). He reflected that "there still exists considerable controversy about whether or not envy is a primary aggressive impulse" (p. 172). Berke tells us that "sufficient evidence does exist to confirm the potentiality for envious attack from birth" (Restak, 1982, pp. 59–60). Further attesting to envy's primacy, he reminds us that Schoeck (1966) has pointed out that while all languages include a concept that embraces envy, not all cultures develop concepts for hope, love, justice and progress:

> Virtually all people, including the most primitive, have found it necessary to define the state of mind of a person who cannot bear someone else's being something, having a skill, possessing something or enjoying a reputation which he himself lacks, and who will therefore rejoice should the other lose his assets, although that loss will not mean his own gain.
>
> (Schoeck, 1966, p. 8)

Berke also conceives of envy as an emotion that begs for disguise and discretion, lest the bearer of envy face the threat of censure or even devastating retaliation. Berke cites Farber (1976), who very eloquently captured this facet of envy: "Envy, by its very nature, is obstinate in its opposition to investigation" (p. 36). He also tells us that envy is "a feared inferiority associated with a sense of unjust deprivation" (p. 180). Berke's definition of envy referenced earlier in this book ("envy is tension aroused by the awareness of vitality and prosperity, indeed, by life itself") impugns envy as a form of psychic energy that acts in the service of death rather than the life instinct, wherein "the duality, life/death, can best be understood as a struggle between forces aiming at growth, order, integration and structure (an upper energy flow) and forces leading to contraction, disorder, fragmentation and chaos (a downward spiral)" (p. 172). Envy, then, is seen as an act of almost pure destructiveness, a means of pulling down and tearing apart that which is alive and vital. It is in this context that Berke pairs narcissism with envy ("narcissism begets envy" p. 182).

In this very powerful passage, Berke makes it disturbingly clear how closely entwined the dynamics of envy and narcissism are:

> The envier is likely to use the very mechanism of envy, powerful projective processes, in order to dissociate himself from a major part of himself, his own destructiveness. In these circumstances an individual may not just project a malign spirit, badness, to attack the animate object, but to get rid of the anguished and envious side of himself, which had initiated the attack in the first place. The result is a loss of self experienced as an increasing inner impoverishment. This loss stimulates murderous rage because the more impoverished the envier feels, the more angry he gets with others (with whom he compares himself) and the more angry he gets with himself (for hating, and for feeling so empty). Moreover, the world (inner or outer reality), becomes suffused with dissociated destructiveness and readily becomes a bad and threatening place. Hence envy gives a paranoid flavor to existence. Instead of desiring life, the envier comes to fear it. (p. 176)

One hears in the above passage most of the major elements that define the narcissist's relationship with himself and with the world at large. I would reiterate that the projective processes that Berke refers to are not all unconsciously motivated, but, rather more frequently than we might wish to acknowledge, consciously directed ones that are meant to infiltrate the other with malevolence, retaliatory rage, and terror to disorganize them, to better justify one's rapacity, and to rob the other of their humanity. The decency that the other possessed that provoked intolerable envy in the narcissist becomes increasingly muted, thereby mitigating envy, but at the cost of constructing a paranoid world in which the narcissist feels himself beset by enemies both within (all the bad objects piling up inside) and without.

In some respects, however, I see the pathological narcissist's envious, retaliatory attacks not so much as a defense meant to relieve envy but, rather, as an inevitable consequence of a life posture that shuts down rewarding and necessary social intercourse with others – wherein intractable withdrawal from the world of relationships is meant to protect the self from the devastating incursions and violations that the narcissist has had to endure as part of the destructive relational systems that characterized his childhood and even later years. My strong sense is, "how could it be otherwise?" As the self pulls away from the people around it, building walls of contempt, mistrust, and withering cynicism to ensure that the self cannot be touched by others, it creates conditions for its own starvation, laying the groundwork for an inner life that is ravaged, desolate, frightening, and increasingly lifeless. Increasingly lifeless, in turn, must generate envy as the self must confront the relatively greater vitality that defines others (greater spontaneity, playfulness, warmth, receptivity to others' experience, empathy, etc. etc.). Such a self must also become aware that others possess the capacity to love and to be authentic. In order to survive and to insulate itself from the violation it expects the world to direct towards it if it foregoes its rigid adherence to strength, it must turn away from love and interconnectedness, prompting my colleague Ian Hughes to conclude, as previously noted, that evil could be defined as envy of love (private communication). The foregoing framework, which I have just outlined, also prompted me to recognize (again, as previously noted) that narcissism serves as a defense against love – as a means to keep the self unencumbered by obligation or ties of affection that might deny it the prerogatives of its ruthless defenses and expose it to catastrophic injury/violation relatedness could occasion.

Berke went on to extend his conception of envy in some important ways: "… excessive projection of destruction also leads to a disturbance in introjection. It, too, may become excessive, as the envier, trying to compensate for his inner emptiness, savagely sucks, bites, and swallows whatever catches his eye. This explains why greed, destructive introjection, is often the companion of envy, destructive projection" (p. 176).

"An envy induced negativity especially interferes with the capacity to receive and return love… This has a disastrous effect on learning… The envier concludes that everything (on the outside) is 'shit,' and that ideas or knowledge, like (envied) food and feelings, are poisonous. So are the relationships which provided them…" (p. 176).

In these passages, Berke recapitulates the tragic consequences that grow out of narcissistic defenses. Such defenses can be seen to exacerbate the foundational experience of envy that is the inescapable progeny of pathological narcissism.

Now, I would like to turn our attention towards narcissism as a defense against fragmentation and dissolution of the self. Writing in 1975, Stolorow identified several authors (Arlow & Brenner, 1964; Kernberg, 1970; Murray, 1964; Oremland & Windholz, 1971) who conceived of "grandiose fantasies of magical omnipotence and un-limited entitlement" (p. 181) as a means of both repairing self-esteem and warding off personal disintegration. Kernberg's formulation, of course, at this point in the book has already been clearly drawn. Fos-sati, Feeney, Pincus, Borroni and Maffei (2015) speculated that nar-cissistic investment in a predominantly grandiose position probably served the function of protecting the self from a confrontation with its most profound fears and the well of negative emotions that its gran-diosity allowed it to contain. Berke suggested that when one is con-sumed with narcissistic pain, omnipotence is equated with goodness, adding that "any omnipotence will do, whether creative or destructive, libidinal or anti-libidinal. The person postulates it as a source of all life and goodness..." (p. 183). Importantly, later in his discussion he suggests that failure of narcissistic defenses that include omnipotence and an inflated sense of self could result in the emergence of powerful suicidal feelings that could lead to loss of life. His views are very close to my own and to Coline Covington's (2023) as well as, I would think, Otto Kernberg's. Kohut also addressed the issue of grandiosity and personal disintegration, but in a context of (as I have understood it) a focus on largely vulnerable narcissistic experience rather than grandi-ose narcissism. It is my belief that the more intractable the investment in grandiosity, the greater the risk of suicide when grandiosity is suc-cessfully challenged and deconstructed (see, for example, Wood, 2023, in press).

And, finally, I want to mention Ferruta and Carmody's poignant characterization of narcissistic inaccessibility as "a defense against wounds which will not heal..." (2012, p. 27). I think this phrase cap-tures the intensity and ferocity of injury that people who become path-ological narcissists endure, prompting them to decisively and indelibly turn away from the world of people.

While there is no opportunity in this short format book to exten-sively consider a subject like etiology, I would like, however briefly, to focus on this topic. Diamond, Yeomans, Stern, and Kernberg (2022) explore this subject in some depth. Their ideas are well worth examining.

Berke (1985), again, also provided a useful formulation of etiology, conveying that "world destroying rage can follow deprivation or gratification… These feelings can be made much worse by a narcissistic parent who treats their children as extension of their own needs in ways that are exceedingly frustrating… suffuse(ing) (them) with desires that cannot be contained and which have to be denied in order to prevent a state of fragmentation and confusion" (p.182). Add to this parental portrait people who imbue their child with lavish attention to the child's inherent gifts, which may be confirmed by imposing congenital assets, and one has created a recipe for the child to make an investment in grandiosity. The sustenance that grandiosity provides serves to offset the terrible deprivation that the child must endure (see, for example, Kernberg, 1970; Wood, 2023). Wood also foresees circumstances in which an emaciated self that had faced repeated violation by predatory parents might seize upon an identification with the narcissistic other if the narcissistic parent enabled and supported it. Such a process would have to be underpinned by an array of personal assets that allowed the child to consummate narcissistic prerogatives. The individual who emerges from either process would be one deeply frightened by interdependence on others, expecting invasion and exploitation rather than nurturance and love.

Shaw (2013) also conceived of pathological narcissism as a response to extensive relational trauma, as did Wood (2023). The implication of a trauma model is that an affected individual can be expected to re-enact their trauma in a way and in forms that potentially allow one penetrating insights into the nature of the psychological injuries that they endured. This was the premise of the work that Wood later did as he attempted to investigate the origins of Vladimir Putin's destructive narcissistic posture. It is, in some ways, very similar to the premises which underlie transference-focused psychotherapy which the Weill Cornell group has developed.

The clear implications of our collective work on both healthy narcissism and pathological narcissism are that in order for us to flourish in our lives we need to be interconnected with one another and we need to be able to emerge from our maturational experiences with our capacity both to give love and to be loved relatively intact. For that to happen, we need to feel welcomed into the human community and we need to feel valued and celebrated, perhaps even in a modestly disproportionate way, much as the social psychological research I cited earlier in this book would seem to suggest. I remember reading a paper

very early on in my career by Ellie Markson, a senior analyst practic-
ing in Toronto in the mid-70s. Ellie emphasized how important it is
for each of us to feel that we are possessed of the capacity to inspire
joy and love in others and act as a source of meaning and inspiration
for them – offering us confirmation that we can touch others and that
we are defined by what I call emotional poignancy. His paper has had
a profound impact on the way I practice, but was lost to me years and
years ago somewhere along the way in the changes of residence that
I have made. Efforts to relocate the paper have all been unsuccessful.
Ellie was the mentor of the two men who mentored me, Paul Lerner
and Ray Freebury, during my postgraduate years.

As I watch my wife's great-granddaughter, who is now slightly
older than 14 months, entrance and delight everyone around her with
her various antics and flirtations, and as I see the pleasure that people
experience in response, I think I have some measure of what we all
require in the very beginning of our lives and, to some degree, in an
ongoing way during the rest of our lives. Under these conditions, our
humanity and our individuality (or our uniqueness, if one likes) are
well-positioned to enhance our own generativity and that of the people
that we touch with our lives and ourselves. This, so far as I can see, is
the magical elixir – the nature of the recognition that we crave – that
we all need if we are to more or less thrive in the face of life's adversi-
ties. The more we are exposed to privation, economic inequality, social disruption and displacement, psychological abuse and neglect, and
cultural forms that demand insensitivity to the pressing psychological
realities that define us, the more prominent our dark side becomes and
the more easily we will wound and damage one another.

References

Arlow, J., & Brenner, C. (1964). *Psychoanalytic concepts and the structural
    theory*. International Universities Press.

Berke, J. (1985). Envy loveth not: A study of the origin, influence and confluence
    of envy and narcissism. *British Journal of Psychotherapy*, *1*(3), 171–186.

Covington, C. (2023). Empire of lies. In *Who's to blame? Collective guilt on
    trial*. Routledge.

Diamond, D., Yeomans, F. E., Stern, B. L., & Kernberg O. F. (2022). *Treating
    pathological narcissism with transference-focused psychotherapy*. The
    Guilford Press.

Elder, P. (1986). Kleinian developments in the concept of narcissism. *British
    Journal of Psychotherapy*, *3*(1), 65–71.

Ferruta, A., & Carmody, C. (2012). Continuity or discontinuity between healthy and pathological narcissism. *Italian Psychoanalytic Annual*, *6*, 19–33.

Fossati, A., Feeney, J., Pincus, A., Borroni, S., & Maffei, C. (2015). The structure of pathological narcissism and its relationships with adult attachment styles. *Psychoanalytic Psychology*, 32(3), 403–431.

Freud, S. (1915). Instincts and their vicissitudes. In Strachey J. (Ed.) *The standard edition of the complete psychological works of Sigmund Freud*, Vol. 14, 343–356.

Gabbard, G. (1993). On hate in love relationships: The narcissism of minor differences revisited. *The Psychoanalytic Quarterly*, *62*, 229–238.

Kernberg, O. (1970). Factors in the treatment of narcissistic personalities. *Journal of the American Psychoanalytic Association*, *18*, 51–85.

Klein, M. (1957). Envy and gratitude. In *The writings of Melanie Klein* (Vol. III). Hogarth Press.

Murray, J. (1964). Narcissism and the ego ideal. *Journal of the American Psychological Association*, *12*, 477–511.

Oremland, J., & Windholz, E. (1971). Some specific transference, countertransference and supervisory problems in the analysis of a narcissistic personality. *International Journal of Psychoanalysis*, *52*, 267–275.

Restak, R. (1982). Newborn knowledge. *Science*, *82*(3), 58–65.

Rosenfeld, H. (1971). A clinical approach to the psychoanalytic theory of life and death instincts: An investigation into the aggressive aspects of narcissism. *International Journal of Psychoanalysis*, *52*(2), 169–178.

Schoeck, H. (1966). *Envy: A theory of social behavior*. Harcourt.

Segal, H. (1983). Some clinical implications of Melanie Klein's work. *International Journal of Psychoanalysis*, *64*, 269–276.

Seidler, G. (1999). Destructive narcissism and the obliteration of self-object separation: Various manifestations of an underlying psychodynamic configuration. *British Journal of Psychotherapy*, *15*(93), 229–305.

Shaw, D. (2013). *Traumatic narcissism; Relational systems of subjugation*. Routledge.

Spillius, E. (1983). Some developments from the work of Melanie Klein. *International Journal of Psychoanalysis*, *64*, 321–332.

Stolorow, R. D. (1975). The narcissistic function of masochism (and sadism). *International Journal of Psychoanalysis*, *56*, 441–448.

Wood, R. (2023). *A study of malignant narcissism: Personal and professional insights*. Routledge.

Wood, R. (Ed.) (in press). *Psychoanalytic reflections on Vladimir Putin: The cost of malignant leadership*. Routledge.

Index

For Product Safety Concerns and Information please contact our EU
representative GPSR@taylorandfrancis.com Taylor & Francis Verlag GmbH,
Kaufingerstraße 24, 80331 München, Germany

Printed and bound by CPI Group (UK) Ltd, Croydon, CR0 4YY
08/06/2025
01897000-0003